Stanisława Byra / Zenon Gajdzica

Teachers' Beliefs about Inclusive Education

A Study in the Context of Major Increases in
Refugee Learners

V&R unipress

Bibliographic information published by the Deutsche Nationalbibliothek
The Deutsche Nationalbibliothek lists this publication in the Deutsche Nationalbibliografie;
detailed bibliographic data are available online: https://dnb.de.

The first research measurement was carried out as part of a project financed by the Ministry of
Education within the project entitled: A study of the practice of mainstream primary schools focused
on implementing inclusive education assumptions. Agreement no. MEN/2020/DWKI/524.
The authors thank the Ministry of Science and Education for its support in the collection of data in
the second measurement conducted in 2022.

Printed and bound by CPI books GmbH, Birkstraße 10, 25917 Leck, Germany
Printed in the EU.

Vandenhoeck & Ruprecht Verlage | www.vandenhoeck-ruprecht-verlage.com

ISBN 978-3-8471-1724-7

Contents

Introduction   9

Chapter 1. Essence and contextuality of inclusive education   11

Chapter 2. Selected contexts and determinants of the transformations of
inclusive education in Poland   21

Chapter 3. Own research concept   27
  Key research assumptions   28
  Data collection and analysis method   29
  Participants and procedure   30
    Instruments   30
    Description of the study group   31

Chapter 4. Teachers' beliefs about the validity of education for all   35
  Validity of education for all – comparative analysis of 2020 and 2022
  study results   35
  Beliefs of the teachers surveyed in 2020 – importance of
  sociodemographic as well as job- and employment-specific variables . .   38
  Beliefs of the teachers surveyed in 2022 – importance of
  sociodemographic as well as job- and employment-specific variables . .   50
  Conclusion and discussion   55

Chapter 5. Learners' subjectivity in inclusive education as rated by
teachers   61
  Learners' subjectivity as rated by teachers – comparative analysis of
  2020 and 2022 study results   61
  Learners' subjectivity as rated by the teachers surveyed in 2020 –
  importance of sociodemographic as well as job- and
  employment-related variables   63

Learners' subjectivity as rated by the teachers surveyed in 2022 – importance of sociodemographic as well as job- and employment-related variables 66
Conclusion and discussion 71

Chapter 6. Support for education/in inclusive education as rated by teachers 75
Supporting learners' learning as rated by teachers – comparative analysis of 2020 and 2022 study results 75
Support of learners' learning and of staff involved in inclusive education as rated by the teachers surveyed in 2020 – importance of sociodemographic as well as job- and employment-related variables . . 79
Support of learners' learning and of staff involved in inclusive education as rated by the teachers surveyed in 2022 – importance of sociodemographic as well as job- and employment-related variables . . 91
Conclusion and discussion 99

Chapter 7. Leadership or collaboration/partnership? Teachers' point of view 103
Collaboration in inclusive education as rated by teachers – comparative analysis of 2020 and 2022 study results 103
Collaboration and leadership as rated by teachers surveyed in 2020 – importance of sociodemographic as well as job- and employment-related variables 108
Collaboration and leadership as rated by the teachers surveyed in 2022 – importance of sociodemographic as well as job- and employment-related variables 121
Conclusion and discussion 129

Chapter 8. Impact of diverse learner needs on the curriculum – teachers' rating 133
Curriculum in inclusive education as rated by teachers – comparative analysis of 2020 and 2022 study results 133
Curriculum in inclusive education as rated by the teachers surveyed in 2020 – importance of sociodemographic as well as job- and employment-related variables 135
Curriculum in inclusive education as rated by the teachers surveyed in 2022 – importance of sociodemographic as well as job- and employment-related variables 137
Conclusion and discussion 142

Research limitations 145

Conclusion 147

References 153

Annex 165
  Raising Achievement Self-Review. Self-review survey 165
    Data protection statement 165
    Instructions for completing the survey 165
  Section 1 – Background information 166
  Section 2 – Inclusive pedagogy 166
    Pedagogy for all learners 166
    Support for learning 167
  Section 3 – Leadership and collaboration 168
    Leadership roles and approaches 168
    Learner well-being and participation 169
    Curriculum development 170
    Partnerships and collaborative working 171
    Support systems for staff and leaders 172

Introduction

Inclusive education is currently not only one of the main currents in the field of education of learners with special developmental needs, but also an important factor in changing whole educational systems, oriented towards improving the quality of education and teaching for all learners. It is therefore not surprising that researchers are particularly interested in the determinants of its quality. Multiple studies have focused on teachers – their competencies to work with a group of learners with diverse abilities and needs, and their attitudes towards the assumptions underlying inclusive education and the ways of implementing it. An analysis of a number of studies shows that teachers' positive attitudes towards inclusive education increase the acceptance of diversity in school, and lead to the construction of favourable solutions in the field (Romi & Leyser, 2006) as well as to the intensification of inclusive practices (Sharma & Sokal, 2016), which ultimately contributes to a successful outcome of this approach (Monsen et al., 2014).

Teachers' attitudes towards inclusive education have many determinants (Guillemot et al., 2022), most of them subject to transformations, which encourages researchers to always continue their explorations, identifying new and updating previously identified factors. The attitudes of teachers towards high quality education for all learners presented and considered in the book fit within these trends. Although the research was carried out on a group of Polish teachers, it shows trends typical of many other countries and therefore provides universal knowledge. However, it also includes unique factors such as the sudden emergence of a large group of refugee children from Ukraine in the education system, as well as the announcement of a radical system reform model by the Ministry of Science and Education.

The main aim of the research presented in this book is to find out about the opinions (expressed by the degree of acceptance) of Polish teachers working at mainstream schools and pre-schools on selected assumptions and organisational solutions underlying inclusive education, and to examine these opinions in terms of selected demographic traits of teachers: gender, place of residence, seniority/ length of service and the level of education taught (pre-school, primary school levels 1 to 3, primary school levels 4 to 8, secondary school) and the type of facility (state, non-state).

An important aim also involves identifying the opinions studied in a temporal perspective – in two measurements (2020 and 2022), making it possible to capture the transformations in the area of acceptance of selected theoretical and organisational assumptions underlying inclusive education. It is worth emphasising at this point that longitudinal studies of teachers' attitudes towards inclusive education are virtually absent from the literature (Guillemot et al., 2020), which we believe makes the results presented here even more interesting.

Chapter 1.
Essence and contextuality of inclusive education

In seeking the non-educational roots of inclusive education, it is worth tracing them back to two historical references. The first one is associated with the social protests of disadvantaged groups, including persons with disabilities. The aim of these protests was, among other things, to obtain equal/fair access to education in mainstream schools (Barnartt & Scotch, 2002). The other reference is the Holocaust, i.e. the mass extermination of people deemed deviant and/or socially undesirable by Nazi Germany. As a corollary of collective historical memory, actions are recognised aimed at creating a tolerant society that is open to diversity (Wagner, 2018). As a result, we can seek the origins of inclusive education in the struggle for recognition and in the perspective of coexistence and respect for diversity (Gajdzica, 2022).

It is generally accepted that the beginnings of inclusive education should be linked to the social activism of parents of children with disabilities in the Nordic countries in the 1960s and 1970s (Dyson & Forlin, 1999). Parents dissatisfied with segregated education demanded that their children be integrated into mainstream education in regular schools, so that they could benefit from equal educational opportunities (Walton,2018). The term "inclusive education" appeared in the educational literature in the early 1990s and quickly gained popularity in countries of the Global North, in particular in Canada and the USA (Szumski, 2019).

Many studies on inclusive education contain the assertion that the very term "inclusion", as applied to the processes of education and learning, is vague, ambiguous, and even controversial (Ryndak et al., 2000; Speck, 2013; Lechta, 2016). Consequently, the concept of inclusive education (educational inclusion) happens to be used in various connotations, with the following meanings: scientific theory, concept of educational transformations, educational model, concept of methodological work, concept of organisational work, set of educational conditions, paradigm, and even ideology (Loreman, 2017; Gajdzica, 2020; Gordon-Gould & Hornby, 2023). It should therefore come as no surprise that inclusive education in practice is an internally diverse and still controversial concept (Mitchell, 2006). This is a result of the circumstances of its parallel construction in many cultures and educational systems (Dyson & Millward, 2000; Loreman, 2017). Although there is relative consensus in the area of the ethical and axiological foundations (equity, equality, value of diversity, etc.), divergences emerge in the area of the praxeological (and therefore also organisational and methodological) premises underlying inclusive education. As a result, many currents can be discerned within it that evolve over time, and that are more or less typical of the space of different educational cultures (Mazurek & Winzer, 1994; Zamkowska, 2004; Mitchell, 2005; Hornby, 2014; Gajdzica et al., 2020). This, in turn, entails divergent concepts of school and of its broadly defined culture of inclusion.

The wealth of connotations and views of inclusive education encourages attempts to classify them. We present several selected suggestions for distinguishing currents/concepts of inclusive education in the section that follows, hoping that they can provide a good introduction, contributing to a better understanding of our research presented in the book. The starting point is provided by the analysis by Mel Ainscow and Susie Miles, who identified the following five perspectives under the term of educational inclusion:
- disability and "special educational needs",
- disciplinary exclusions,
- groups vulnerable to exclusion,
- the promotion of a school for all,
- education for all (Ainscow & Miles, 2008).

Although the diagnosed typology of research fields consists of inseparable areas, it nevertheless makes it possible to view the topic of our research systemically. The first three areas refer to particular groups of learners being included, whereas the last two areas show the inclusion perspective as a strategy for changing education, school, and the culture surrounding it. Although in many parts of the book we focus on learners with disabilities (this group continues to be the main beneficiary of inclusion processes in many currents), our interest remains centred primarily on schools and on quality education for all.

Despite the multifaceted diversity, some generalisations can be made in the area of the transformations of inclusive education. Kerstin Göransson and Claes Nilholm (2014) identified and described these developments on the basis of a review of the definitions of inclusive education. The research they presented concerns inclusion of learners with disabilities, but the mechanisms of change they described can equally well be applied to a broad form of inclusive education that includes all learners belonging to socially underprivileged groups and/or having learning difficulties for a variety of reasons. As a result of their analyses, Kerstin Göransson and Claes Nilholm (2014) distinguished four categories of definitions reflecting the stages of inclusive education transformations. We supplement their presentation with our own comments and references to the literature.

The basic premise underlying the first group of definitions involves mainstreaming of learners with disabilities. Although, according to the cited authors, few researchers explicitly suggest the category of place as a fundamental aspect of educational inclusion, it does play a key role in many definitions and is the first feature to be mentioned. Furthermore, this education should take place in groups of learners of the same biological age and be characterised by support given to the learners being included. An example of this approach is the definition presented in the *Concise Encyclopedia of Special Education* (Reynolds & Flechter-Janzen, 2002, p. 495), which identifies several key assumptions that form the foundations underlying inclusive education, namely:

– placing learners with disabilities in general education classrooms;
– educating learners with disabilities with learners of the same age who do not have disabilities;
– including all learners in the mainstream of education using special support;
– belonging of all learners to the school community.

In its centre, the second group of definitions has the special needs of the learners being included and the process of meeting these needs. Their impact on the education of other learners is, in turn, marginalised. An example of inclusive education understood in this manner is the approach of David Mitchell (2008), who sees it as educating people with special educational needs in a typical school environment. In this view, inclusive education is more than merely placing the group of learners being integrated in the space of a mainstream school, as it also means implementing a whole set of rules, changes in curricula and teaching methods, as well as adjustments to assessment techniques and accessibility rules (Mitchell, 2016). This, in turn, requires appropriate teacher support in the classroom space. Inclusive education is therefore a complex strategy aimed primarily at mainstreaming learners with disabilities (Gajdzica, 2020).

Supporting learners with special educational needs (the concept of special needs being typical of the first two groups of definitions) taking place in the space of a mainstream school/classroom is not without effect on the other learners. As a result of this, it has been noted that inclusive education cannot be considered globally as an organisational form covering only the learners being mainstreamed. Consequently, the next group of definitions approaches inclusive education from the point of view of each learner. This, on its part, leads to the recognition of the individual needs of all learners – including those with relatively normal development and socialisation. These definitions place the form of

education and learning being discussed in the broader context of general education. The following assumptions sum up this approach:
- inclusive education makes the school a place of education for all children;
- inclusive education meets the needs of every learner in a better way;
- inclusive education is a process aimed at seeking the most normal educational pathways possible for all children (Thomazet, 2009, after: Göransson & Nilholm, 2014, p. 269).

An example of such an approach can also be found in the *Model of Education for All* (2020) designed in Poland, according to which inclusive education should be understood as "quality education for all children, pupils and adult learners, organised together with their peers in the place where they live. High quality implies both the active involvement and participation of each child/learner in the teaching/learning process, social inclusion, as well as progress in individual development and educational outcomes" (*Model edukacji dla wszystkich*, 2020, p. 21).

The three groups of definitions are descriptive in their nature, as they describe the forms of educational organisation existing in practice (Szumski, 2019). The last group, presented below, is characterised by its projective and prescriptive nature. The definitions classified in this group are aimed at constructing organisational visions of education for all, as suggested by the title. Concepts of inclusive education understood in this way highlight a community built on an inclusive culture. The culture of such a community is to be based on diversity, on the nurturing of equality and equity, and on the removal of all barriers to inclusion, which operates in a natural way (Göransson & Nilholm, 2014). Thus, the category of inclusion loses its raison d'être because there is only one current of education that includes all learners (Thomas & Loxley, 2007; Slee, 2011). As a result, there can be no talk of any group of learners being included, as no marginalising/exclusionary practices are in operation. The vision expressed in this group of definitions discussed above is sometimes described as a postulate of absolutisation, far removed from reality and in practice considered unrealistic by some researchers (Speck, 2013).

It is difficult to unequivocally place the current Polish inclusive education in this typology. On the one hand, educational practice continues to show that its practical implementation is very deeply rooted in the assumptions of special pedagogy. This is reflected in the definitions, focusing mainly on recognising the needs of the learners being included. On the other hand, there are increasingly clear symptoms of this area being treated as an immanent field of education in a broad sense, with an emphasis on the individual needs of all learners (Gajdzica et al., 2021).

Among the many concepts of identifying the currents/types of inclusive education present in the literature, it is worth pointing to yet another differentiating criterion. It involves the relationship of inclusive education to special education. Although in practice these currents interpenetrate and remain in many aspects convergent, the theoretical positions demonstrate divergences in terms of the following: references to propositions developed in the context of special education, ontological and paradigmatic assumptions for the practice of teaching, and, as a result, also the key categories constituting the conceptual foundations. Generally, the first concept assumes that inclusive education is a continuation (sometimes referred to as a superstructure) of special education (Lechta, 2016; Loreman, 2017; Gajdzica, 2020). This usually leads to the recognition of the co-existence of both types of education and different learning pathways for learners with special educational needs (Hornby, 2020). As a result of these assumptions, it can be described as reconstructive inclusive education (reconstructing the assumptions underlying special education and adapting them to the realities of a mainstream school). The second current assumes that it should be completely divergent from the assumptions of special education. This, in turn, leads to an emphasis placed in practice on a single educational pathway for all learners (Thomas & Loxley, 2007; Slee, 2011). Therefore, it constitutes deconstructive inclusive education (rejecting the assumptions developed in special education and building new principles for inclusion into mainstream schools).

The main differentiating criteria are listed in Table 1.

Table 1. Theoretical presentation of the differences between reconstructive and deconstructive inclusion

Distinguishing criterion	Reconstructive inclusion	Deconstructive inclusion
Attitudes towards the assumptions underlying special education	Continuation / super-structure / modification	Rejection
Paradigmatic rooting	Positivist (structural-functional)	Interpretative (constructivist, critical)
Embedment in didactics	Instructional / normative	Constructivist / critical
Key categories	Disability, special educational needs, specialist support, mainstream, adaptation, specialist teacher competencies	Diversity, equal access, equity, school for all, mainstream curriculum, inclusive school culture, barriers
Contextual categories	Nearest environment (in this approach: that of the local area mainstream school), individualisation, barrier, school for all, human rights	Educational current, personalisation, teachers' competencies to work with a heterogeneous group

Table 1 *(Continued)*

Distinguishing criterion	Reconstructive inclusion	Deconstructive inclusion
Key feature	Bringing together in one space two cultures of education: special and mainstream – creating a borderland culture	Building a new, original culture
Perspective on the learner	Functional and social	Social
Organisational goal	Mainstreaming	Removing barriers
Perception of educational needs	Special and shared	Different – personalised ways of meeting all needs
Approach to the education system	Pluralistic (one of many forms of education)	Rejection of educational pluralism (the only form of education)

(own compilation based on: Mäller et al., 2004; Topping & Maloney, 2005; Allan, 2007; Thomas & Loxley, 2007; Zacharuk, 2008; Loreman, 2009; Zamkowska, 2009; Slee, 2011; Kruk-Lasocka, 2012; Speck, 2013; Bartoňová, 2014; Peng & Potměšil, 2015; Lechta, 2016; Sadowska, 2018; Gajdzica. 2020; Nadachowicz & Bilewicz, 2020).

Naturally, in practice it is difficult to find pure forms of concepts defined in such a specific manner. They do not usually appear in explicit formulas, so the juxtapositions presented within one and the other concept should be perceived as idealistic and projective. Nevertheless, the collation of the categories presented in the table makes it possible to show the divergences within inclusive education, which encourages a somewhat more detailed characterisation of reconstructive and deconstructive inclusion.

The concept conventionally referred to as reconstructive inclusive education represents a certain continuation and superstructure of special education. It is based on an evolution of the assumptions underlying special pedagogy and on reconstructing them for the purposes of inclusive education – in other words, on their adaptation to the conditions of a mainstream school. As a result (despite the absence of such declarations on the part of its authors), it refers, in many of its foundations, to the culture of special education (involving separation/segregation) with the premise of modifying its organisational assumptions. Thus, the key categories building the concept of reconstructive inclusion are those typical of special pedagogy (disability, special educational needs, specialist support, individualisation, specialist teacher competencies) supplemented by categories related to mainstream education (the nearest environment, school for all, equal access). The two groups are bonded together by the categories of mainstream, barriers, and adaptation. This approach manifests itself more often in selected elements of the concept of educational inclusion designed in Central European countries, including Poland (Zacharuk, 2008; Zamkowska, 2009; Kruk-Lasocka, 2012; Speck, 2013; Peng & Potměšil, 2015; Lechta, 2016).

One of the typical features of this current is the juxtaposition of two cultures of education, special and mainstream, within one space. In this framework, learners with special needs remain influenced by the former, and the other learners – by the latter. The contamination of both areas of education requires some structuring, hence the importance gained by the concept of special educational needs (along with disability and/or other difficulties and limitations related to them within the scope discussed) and by the mainstream of work. The theoretical foundations of educating a learner with special needs are embedded in the body of work of special pedagogy. The essence of mainstream education, in turn, is based on premises developed on the basis of general pedagogy, including in particular general didactics and teaching methodologies. This tradition provides a body of experience rooted in positivist currents of practising science, above all in quasi-behavioural, instructional, and normative didactics (Gajdzica, 2020).

Although inclusive education understood in this way is declaratively linked above all to the social model of disability, it rests in many aspects upon functional assumptions, which in turn form the basis for perceiving special educational needs and individualising work with learners with special educational needs (Mäller et al., 2004; Bartoňová, 2014; Lechta, 2016; Nadachowicz & Bilewicz, 2020).

The sets of conceptual assumptions underlying educational inclusion understood in this way usually open with the word "all" – e.g., all children attend the nearest (local area) school, all children study in regular classrooms with their peers, all learners are valued, all children follow similar curricula, all children are supported, etc. (Topping & Maloney, 2005, p. 6; Loreman, 2009, p. 43). Another feature of the concepts discussed here involves the notions used: the inclusion of all learners in mainstream education, the belonging of all learners to the school community (Reynolds & Flechter-Janzen, 2002, p. 495; Topping & Maloney, 2005, p. 6).

The primary aim of inclusion is identified with educational mainstreaming. The objective, therefore, is to make sure that all learners (regardless of their limitations and abilities) can participate fully in the classroom and school community. In this approach, mainstream educational activities are defined by the mainstream school category. In the case of class work, the mainstream represents the fundamental point of reference for all organisational processes. For example, organising class work in line with the co-teaching strategy, an alternative teaching technique, implies the functioning of two streams: a mainstream and a sidestream (Friend, Cook, Hurley-Chamberlain, & Shamberger, 2010, p. 12). The sidestream generally includes learners who require special support, the intensity of which usually makes integration into mainstream class work difficult. Naturally, specifying the mainstream class work in more detail involves having clear assumptions and remains linked to the category of participation.

Participation includes not only physical presence in the space of a mainstream school, but also active contribution to classroom activities, work on the tasks performed in the course of education, cooperation in problem solving, meeting individual and group needs, participation in school culture, and building the latter (Gajdzica, 2020).

The second concept, conventionally referred to as deconstructive educational inclusion, refers in its strategic assumptions above all to the identification and removal of barriers and of exclusionary/marginalising factors in education (Slee, 2011), and in this respect also of the practices of imposing a framework of desirable development on learners that reinforces marginalising tendencies (Slee, 2014).

Important categories building this concept include diversity, equal access, equity, school for all, mainstream curriculum, barriers, and inclusive school culture (Allan, 2007; Thomas & Loxley, 2007; Slee, 2011; Sadowska, 2018). The basis underlying the design of this concept is dissociation from the legacy of special education. In fact, it is a form of education largely based on a criticism of special education (of its contradictions, weaknesses, selectivity, neophytism of individualisation, primitive revalidation, glorification of the medical model of disability, segregation/separation practices, etc.) (Gajdzica, 2020). The concept is characterised by the denial of the mechanisms that generate barriers in main-stream education. Furthermore, its origin can be traced to the criticism of the pluralistic (multi-track) approach to the organisation of the education system. The authors of this concept refer exclusively to the social model of disability and rely on the assumptions of constructivist pedagogy. The strategic categories of the deconstructive inclusion definition group are marginalisation/exclusion and barriers. Identification and removal of barriers as well as elimination of the negative processes of marginalisation represent the starting point for creating a genuine culture of inclusive education – laying the foundations for the realisation of the premise of equal participation in education (Allan, 2007; Thomas & Loxley, 2007; Slee, 2011).

The guiding motto in this current is to build an inclusive school culture from the ground up. An inclusive school can be neither a modified special needs school, nor a modified mainstream school. It should be a school without barriers, which in practice are generated not only by the dominant culture (of able-bodiedness/able-mindedness) but also by the dominated culture (of disability). The school dichotomy is therefore not a good solution, according to the repre-sentatives of this current, for the building of a culture of inclusive education. The latter must not involve trying to adjust learners with disabilities to the main-stream education system (Slee, 2004). It should be based on a profound reform of the system and on building a culture of inclusion from the ground up (Slee, 2011).

To recapitulate, the concept is based on a criticism of inclusive mainstream school built on the experiences and traditions of special needs and mainstream education creating a space of a cultural and educational borderland – where various normative regulations, rules of play, cultural codes, etc. co-exist in one area, and where diverse groups, different cultures and expectations clash (Jałowiecki & Karpalski, 2011; Gołdyga, 2013). The concept of deconstructive educational inclusion is thus embedded not only in the idea of deconstructing special education, but also in the rejection of the typical mainstream school culture. Therefore, inclusive education placed in the deconstructive current cannot be built on the foundation of a mainstream school (Thomas & Loxley, 2007), but neither is it a new version of special education. Treating inclusive education in this way would limit its potential and even destroy its innovative nature. Inclusive pedagogy, in a broad sense, should therefore be regarded as a sub-discipline of pedagogy, rather than as a new version of special pedagogy (Hinz, 2009 after: Szumski & Firkowska-Mankiewicz, 2010).

When discussing the educational, social and cultural determinants of the design of both currents, it is worth mentioning that the first one (reconstructive inclusion) refers more to learners with disabilities. Simplifying, one can describe this group as the main beneficiaries of inclusion. The second current (deconstructive inclusion), on the other hand, draws its assumptions more strongly from all possible differences between learners: cultural, religious, gender, economic, and functional ones. Thus, the target group for inclusion consists of all disadvantaged learners: those with core curriculum difficulties, adaptation problems, as well as above-average abilities or talents. It should not be found surprising, therefore, that in countries with less cultural diversity and/or tendencies of resistance against cultural and religious diversity, the dominant approach is associated with the first current. The second current, in turn, is likely to develop more dynamically in countries that are diverse in the respects mentioned above, where cultural and religious diversity is the norm in classrooms, and where gender and social issues are a significant part of the state's social policy.

The proposition formulated above, speculative in its nature, probably requires validation, nevertheless in Central and Eastern European countries (where in practice the indicated intercultural education issues occur less intensely) inclusive tendencies typical of the first current prevail, whereas in Scandinavia, North America, and some Western European countries, the deconstructive current has been developing more vigorously (Gajdzica, 2020).

The cited typologies of inclusive education do not exhaust all of its possible typologies, but they do confirm the proposition formulated earlier, namely that the concept represents an internally diverse, evolving project, rich in various connotations.

In the perspective adopted here, we assume inclusive education to include all the processes and activities aimed at formulating the totality of human capabilities, sensitive to the individual needs of each person regardless of their developmental potential and socialisation skills. We see the learners' identified challenges as a consequence of functional and/or socially constructed disorders. Inclusive education processes take place in non-segregated and non-separated conditions, i.e. in non-categorising circumstances, respecting and taking into account the diverse capacities and needs of the individuals being educated. Its important tasks include increasing social participation, especially of individuals who are developmentally/socially (culturally, economically) disadvantaged, and enhancing the quality of education for all learners, also those with relatively normal development. An essential premise of inclusive education involves anticipating, identifying and eliminating all barriers (mental, cultural, and architectural) that prevent/hinder inclusion processes, as well as creating a culture of working together built on a sense of community, respect, equality, and recognising diversity as a value. We perceive inclusive education as a process that draws on the achievements of various social and human sciences, including special pedagogy, with the aim of reconstructing these outputs to create optimal developmental conditions for all learners in mainstream institutions (Gajdzica, 2020).

Furthermore, we assume that inclusive education is a model that takes a specific organisational form based on constructivist strategies of working with a diverse group in a single current, taking into account processes of supporting all learners and a personalistic approach to the fulfilment of their needs.

Chapter 2.
Selected contexts and determinants of the transformations of inclusive education in Poland

Schools create a microclimate that mirrors social relations, attitudes, as well as rules and norms. The school microclimate represents a compilation of external and internal factors associated with culture. The former represent primarily the social culture around the school, whereas the latter include the institutional culture created within the specific school. School culture is therefore an element of the broad social culture and encompasses the totality of beliefs, views, attitudes, relationships, and principles shaping all aspects of the school's functioning as an institution, organisation, and community (Czerepaniak-Walczak, 2015, p. 80). Therefore, when discussing the context of inclusive education in Poland, it is worth making at least a brief reference to the broader cultural determinants related to multiculturalism, among other things.

Until recently, Poland could hardly be seen as a culturally diverse country. For example, in the National Census (NSP) conducted in 2011, the number of self-declarations of belonging to a national or ethnic minority (except the indications of Silesian nationality, which is not officially recognised in Poland) amounted to only 394,000, which accounted for around one per cent of Poland's population at that time, and included just under 39,000 indications of Ukrainian nationality (*Siódmy raport ...*, 2020, p. 2). In turn, the number of learners within the individual national minorities, ethnic minorities and regional language communities for which an educational subsidy was calculated in the 2017/2018 school year was just under 80,000 (approx. 1.7% of all learners), including slightly over 3,000 Ukrainian learners. (*Siódmy raport...*, 2020, p. 57). The historical origins of this situation can be traced to the migrations of minorities (e. g., the German and the Jewish ones), inhabiting the territory of present-day Poland for many centuries, outside the country's post-war borders, as well as to Poland's isolation and to the unification policy pursued by the communist authorities. Consequently, Poles had negligible relations with immigrants and cultural minorities (including religious and even denominational ones) until the 1990s. Religious diversity is also low in Poland, which in practice impoverishes discourse on refugees and immigrants arriving in Poland (Cekiera, 2022). Cultural transfer, understood as long-term (post-World War Two in this approach) interpenetration of cultural content as a result of the development processes of societies in Poland, was practically absent (Szaban, 2020). The circumstances determining mono-culturalism began to change with the increase in economic migration of Poles after 1989 and the improvement of the standard of living of the Polish pop-ulation, which was also conducive to tourist travel. The second decade of the 21st century saw an influx of economic migration from Asia and Eastern Europe (especially Ukraine). These experiences fostered the creation of "cultural bor-derlands". Unfortunately, increasing multiculturalism also reinforced nation-alist attitudes, typical of far-right social movements (Nikitorowicz, 2017).

The situation changed markedly after the Russian aggression against Ukraine. Researchers investigating migration estimate that more than 1.35 million Ukrainians had already been living in Poland before February 2022, while around 3 million refugees arrived in Poland in the first dozen weeks or so following the invasion (Duszczyk & Kaczmarczyk, 2022; Boroń & Gromkowska-Melosik, 2022). The social structure of the refugee population differed significantly from that of economic migrants before 2022. Ukrainians working in Poland before the war were mostly men, while the refugees arriving after February 2022 were pre-dominantly women, children, and youth, with 26% under the age of 18 (Babińska et al., 2022). This change represented not only a social and economic challenge, but also an educational one. According to data provided by the Ministry of Education and Science, one year after the Russian aggression against Ukraine, 190,000 Ukrainian children were present in Polish pre-schools and schools (*MEiN: W polskich szkołach i przedszkolach,... 2023*).

Poland's low cultural diversity (especially until the end of the 20th century) also influenced, to some extent, attitudes towards people with disabilities, who were often perceived as different, or even alien. Thus, persons with disabilities un-doubtedly experienced a post-colonial policy, based on stereotypes and creating a distance towards the Others. A certain specificity could be noticed here, typical of monocultural communities. It can be described using the following categories:
- negative ones – ignorance, fear, pity, misunderstanding, distancing;
- ambivalent ones – passivity, indifference;
- positive ones – curiosity, solidarity (Gajdzica et al., 2020).

However, it can hardly be argued that the attitudes of Poles towards persons with disabilities were significantly different under real socialism compared to the attitudes of people in other countries. More recent comparative research does not demonstrate particularly significant differences between attitudes in the Polish population and in other countries with regard to the matter (Bera & Korczyński, 2012; Gajdzica, 2013). Nevertheless, assuming that the culture of social and ed-ucational inclusion grows in direct proportion to the cultural diversity within the given community, it needs to be argued that the changes in the Polish society over the recent decades, as described above, have been conducive to the transformation of attitudes towards educational inclusion and building an inclusive school culture.

Four periods can be distinguished following an analysis of the legislation standardising the Polish educational system with regard to learners with special educational needs after the systemic turning point of 1989:

- The first period was that preceding the introduction of legal and formal conditions for inclusive education in 1991. It was a time when segregated education for learners with disabilities prevailed, while other special needs were marginalised.
- The second period, between 1991 and 2010, corresponded to the years of the so-called inclusive education boom. Special educational needs other than those related to disabilities began to be recognised then.
- The third period started in 2010 after the adoption of a package of regulations describing comprehensive changes in the education of learners with special needs and the organisation and provision of psychological and pedagogical assistance to them. At that time, intensified efforts were made to develop inclusive education catering also to learners with special needs other than those related to disabilities (Cytowska, 2016).
- The fourth period started in 2020, when the Ministry of Education announced a plan to build quality education for all learners (*Model edukacji dla wszystkich,* 2020). After heated discussions and a reorganisation of the concept, the change started to be implemented, in small steps, in 2022.

In the 2019/2020 school year, as many as 30% of learners in Poland were covered by various forms of psychological and pedagogical assistance, whereas 70% of learners with a statement of special education needs (mainly due to disabilities) were pursuing compulsory education in mainstream facilities (*Model edukacji dla wszystkich,* 2020, p. 12). Psychological and pedagogical assistance is therefore an important component of the work of mainstream schools. The inclusive form of education for learners with disabilities has become statistically dominant compared to education provided in special institutions. It is worth recalling that although broadly defined inclusive education used to be associated for many years in Poland primarily with learners with disabilities, it also includes other disadvantaged groups (e.g., learners with emotional disorders and partial learning difficulties, children of immigrants and refugees, children growing up in poverty-stricken families, transgender and homosexual learners, and learners with gender identification problems). However, the physical presence of these learners in mainstream schools is not tantamount to the actual implementation of quality inclusive education (Gajdzica, 2022). Research findings indicate that the mainstream schools are insufficiently prepared to deliver inclusive education. A key problem is the low degree of teachers' readiness (negative or ambivalent attitudes) to implement inclusive education (Kołodziejczyk, 2020, Skibska, 2021) and the related insufficient knowledge and methodological competencies (especially in the case of subject teachers) when it comes to working with a diverse group (Janiszewska-Nieścioruk, 2016; Chrzanowska, 2019; Skotnicka, 2019; Gajdzica, 2020). In addition, research findings indicate that teachers are insufficiently prepared for diagnosing learners' special needs (Kochanowska, 2015; Skibska, Borzecka, & Twaróg-Kanus, 2020). According to teachers, other significant problems concern the scarcity of specialists and assistants performing therapeutic and care tasks in a mainstream setting (Skotnicka, 2019; Nowak, 2020) and the lack of organisational and methodological support (Chrzanowska, 2019; Gajdzica, 2020; Nowak, 2020).

Despite the problems indicated above, inclusive education is a rapidly growing form of education in Poland. It is now becoming a catalyst for transformations of the entire education system aimed at improving the quality for all learners, in line with the assumption that every learner has their own personal needs and it is important to meet the latter as fully as possible through a variety of ways, methods, and means.

The SWOT analysis presented below, performed several years ago, summarises to some degree the strengths and weaknesses of inclusive education in Poland as well as the related opportunities and threats. Due to the constant changes and the dynamic surge in interculturalism in Polish schools, the analysis has been supplemented and adapted to match the current reality.

Table 2. SWOT analysis of inclusive education in Poland, from the point of view of culture, conditions, and educational practices

Strengths	Weaknesses
– Increased public awareness of the needs and capabilities of people with disabilities. – Increased public acceptance of inclusive education. – Increased public awareness of parents of learners with disabilities. – Emancipation of milieus of persons with disabilities. – Statistical increase in the number of learners with disabilities taught in mainstream schools.	– Insufficient participation of parents of learners with disabilities and of experts in the creation of educational policy at the national and local level. – Apparent accountability of local governments for spending additional resources on the education of learners with a statement of special education needs. – Insufficient competencies of subject teachers to work with a heterogeneous group.

Table 2 *(Continued)*

Strengths	Weaknesses
– Increased number of mainstream school teachers qualified to work with learners with SEN, especially at the primary school levels 1 to 3 education stage. – Growing number of scientific publications (especially conceptual considerations) on educational inclusion. – Removal of architectural barriers in mainstream schools. – Increased number of good practices in the field of differentiated instruction. – Increased number of NGOs working for school development.	– Ambivalent attitudes of teachers towards inclusive education. – Teachers' mental barriers. – Creation, in practice, of a simplified concept of educational inclusion based on the reconstruction of the assumptions underlying special education. – Underestimation of the role of school culture in creating inclusive education. – Insufficient number of studies on the conditions for educational inclusion. – Insufficient preparation of schools to accommodate learners from Ukrainian refugee families.
Opportunities	Threats
– Strengthened social activity of people with disabilities, parents of learners with disabilities and experts in reforming the special education system. – Increased multiculturalism of society. – Intercultural enrichment of the school related to the enrolment of a significant number of learners from Ukraine. – Development of the concept of inclusive education based on elements of deconstruction of special pedagogy. – Change in the training of mainstream schools teachers: equipping them with competencies to work with a diverse group. – Declining learner numbers (demographic decline), resulting in smaller class size. – Expansion of the base of teaching resources and methodological aids. – Development of a concept for change aimed at supporting inclusive education by the Ministry of Education.	– Political transformations: moving away from democratic standards (also in the area of educational management). – Increase in negative social attitudes towards otherness. – Perceiving inclusion as an ideology. – Political tendencies to return to segregationist practices in the education system. – Ignoring the opinions of experts and parents in the building of an organisational culture of inclusive school. – Economic crisis and perceiving inclusive education as very expensive. – Conservative embeddedness of the school model in instructional didactics. – Continued glorification of the medical model of disability of learners in social practice

(based on: Gajdzica et al., 2020, p. 56).

Reference can be made to several fundamental changes when seeking systemic solutions aimed at transforming the diagnosed state. The first change is related to acquiring/improving the competencies of mainstream school teachers to work with a diverse group. This requires above all a change in the standards of teaching and further training of teachers (especially subject teachers), which continues to encounter resistance especially among political decision-makers. The second change concerns organisational and methodological support for mainstream schools and pre-schools. This is provided for instance by hiring more specialists to work at schools, building a network of institutional support using the potential of special needs schools, and coordinating internal school strategies for working with learners requiring psychological and pedagogical assistance. In practice, this area is linked to the need to create genuine inclusive education leaders in mainstream institutions, but also to orient educational strategies/curricula towards recognising diversity as a value that builds the subjectivity of each learner. The third area discussed concerns persuading teachers to embrace inclusive education, shaping their positive attitude towards this form of education and convincing them to jointly build a school culture for all. We adopted this latter area as the starting point in the analysis of the research findings, treating the other areas as an important complement.

Chapter 3.
Own research concept

The research project presented here fits into two broader thematic areas. The first one involves exploring teachers' attitudes towards specific components of broadly perceived education. The second one involves diagnosing the determinants of high quality education for all learners.

Studying attitudes in the field of special needs education (including non-segregated education) has a rich tradition. This research is carried out in a variety of settings (school and out-of-school), involving diverse groups (teachers, parents, headmasters/headmistresses, learners), and it has been aimed at exploring and examining attitudes towards the numerous different elements, states and processes that make up education in a broad sense. These explorations are of a comparative nature or focus on one specific field. The studies use standardised tools (scales, questionnaires) or non-standardised ones (Gajdzica, 2013; Byra & Domagała-Zyśk, 2021). One form of studying attitudes consists in finding out about the opinions, expressed by the degree of acceptance or negation of certain organisational solutions (e.g., forms of work, educational models, strategies, working methods, etc.) and important assumptions (ethical, organisational, methodological foundations, etc.) underlying a specific educational concept. This form of research usually refers to the emotional component of attitude, and somewhat less frequently to the cognitive or behavioural ones. The vast majority of such explorations are embedded in a positivist paradigm taking the form of quantitative studies making it possible, subject to the standardisation of the tool and careful sampling, to compare data collected in different areas (countries, states) and in different periods of time (repetition of the survey at certain intervals).

In turn, the study of the determinants of effective education for all learners covers many different areas. Teachers' attitudes towards inclusive education are widely regarded as one of the main factors determining the effective implementation of this form of education (Loreman et al., 2014; Guillemot et al., 2022; Lindner et al., 2023). Therefore, the study of teachers' attitudes (in the cognitive, emotional and behavioural components) is one of the richest currents of research on the determinants of the development and effectiveness of inclusive education. However, the rich output provided in this area by Polish researchers (e. g., Gajdzica, 2011a; Barańska & Sirak, 2015; Ćwirynkało & Żyta 2015; Bąbka & Podgruszewska, 2016; Żuraw 2016; Chrzanowska, 2019; Skotnicka, 2019; Skibska, 2021) is not widely shared in the global discourse, as the vast majority of research results have been published in Polish. We seek to fill this gap by presenting our research in this book.

Key research assumptions

The research presented here fits within exploration assumptions:
- embedded in the positivist paradigm,
- involving the investigation of attitudes expressed by the degree of acceptance of selected organisational solutions and assumptions underlying inclusive education,
- aimed at identifying and examining above all the emotional component of the attitude,
- using a standardised tool,
- using a large sample group,
- involving repeating measurements over time, assuming the emergence of a potential determinant of changes in acceptance levels.

The main aim of the research presented here was to find out the opinions (expressed by the degree of acceptance) of mainstream school and pre-schools on selected organisational solutions and assumptions underlying inclusive education.

Another aim of the presented research involves examining the opinions in terms of selected demographic characteristics of teachers: gender, place of residence, seniority/length of service and the level of education taught (pre-school, primary school levels 1 to 3, primary school levels 4 to 8, secondary school) and the institution type (state, non-state).

An important aim involves identifying the opinions studied in a temporal perspective – in two measurements (2020 and 2022), making it possible to capture the transformations in the area of acceptance of selected theoretical and organisational assumptions underlying inclusive education. At this point, it is worth mentioning that the relatively short period between the two measurements was characterised by significant changes in the field of Polish education due to the arrival of a large group of culturally different learners from Ukraine and the publication of draft assumptions for a reform of inclusive education by the Ministry of National Education.

Data collection and analysis method

A longitudinal research strategy was used to collect the data. Longitudinal studies are among the less frequently used methods in pedagogy, which is probably because they are difficult to organise, last longer, and usually cost more compared to cross-sectional studies. They are usually aimed at collecting data showing changes in attitudes and preferences, or at capturing the processual nature of changes in the effects of specific factors. This, in turn, makes them popular mainly in the area of consumer or political research (Johnson et al., 2015).

Dynamic longitudinal research uses mainly the panel technique, whereas tracking studies, also referred to as trend studies (Babbie, 2005; Markens,2003), are rarely used in pedagogy.

In the research project presented here, data were collected using a tracking technique, generally applied when monitoring changes in the attitudes or behaviours of respondents over a longer period of time. The research was conducted in tranches, at cyclical intervals. Each tranche, however, represents a fully independent study of a specific community. All tranches follow the same research concept (Sawiński, 2007). In many assumptions, they are similar to panel surveys. They share the following common features:

- possibility of capturing changes in opinions, attitudes, and behaviours of the group studied,
- repeatability over time,
- using the same (or, as in tracking studies, a similar) tool in subsequent measurements (Sołoma, 2002).

The difference, however, lies in the sampling. In tracking studies, the group is selected separately in each tranche. It includes different (or partly different) respondents (Sawiński, 2007). However, they are an analogous group in terms of their experience (e. g., implementation of the assumptions underlying inclusive education) or traits, the functions performed, and the tasks carried out (e. g., working as teachers in mainstream schools). These are therefore studies that require the participation of a group which has the same characteristics, but is not the same (in terms of the specific individuals) as in the case of panel surveys. A sample that has the same characteristics is understood to consist of a certain number of people with similar traits/attributes (e. g., same gender, age category, education level or other features, relevant to the aspect being examined) (Sołoma, 2005). It is therefore important that the group be selected in each wave of the research on the basis of identical criteria and that the research be conducted under analogous conditions (Dyjas-Pokorska,2005). Such research models tend to be structured in two ways. The first of these reflects the prioritisation of representative cross-sectional studies conducted at specific intervals. The other one involves structuring the indicators into time series already at the initial stage of data presentation (Markens, 2003). Both structuring methods were used in our research project: the data is discussed in a longitudinal perspective (comparing the 2020 and 2022 data) and in a cross-sectional perspective (examining the 2020 and 2022 data separately in terms of selected differentiating variables).

The use of the tracking technique frees the research project from the drawback of sample attrition (Sołoma, 2002), of losing access to the individuals displaying the attitudes studied and to their experience, or of losing contact with the individuals studied, as well as of the latter learning in advance the answers to the questions posed, which may affect measurement reliability (Sawiński, 2007; Gajdzica, 2020). These characteristics of tracking surveys formed the basis underlying their selection for the pursuit of the research objectives formulated.

Participants and procedure

The study covered teachers employed at mainstream state and non-state facilities. The selection criterion was employment at one of the following teaching levels: pre-school, early primary school levels 1 to 3, levels 4 to 8, or all levels, and at secondary school level. The exclusion criterion was employment at inclusive facilities and ones with inclusive classes. The structure of the surveyed groups of teachers, studied in two different time periods (2020 and 2022), was standardised in terms of two converging traits: gender and place of residence. The surveys were conducted using an online platform making it possible to guarantee research anonymity as well as data coding and archiving. The research was carried out in part under a grant funded by the Ministry of Education and Science (*Badanie praktyki ogólnodostępnych szkół podstawowych w zakresie edukacji włączającej* [*Research into the Practice of Mainstream Primary Schools with Regard to Inclusive Education*]), based on guidelines of the European Agency for Special Needs and Inclusive Education.

Instruments

The diagnosed opinions of pre-school and mainstream school teachers concerning selected assumptions and organisational solutions underlying inclusive education were measured using the Polish version (KSPS) of the Raising Achievement Self-Review survey, developed by the project team of the European Agency for Special Needs and Inclusive Education (V.J. Donnelly, Anthoula Kefallinou, 2017). The psychometric properties of the Polish version of the tool were tested in 2020 by a project team led by Zenon Gajdzica, with satisfactory results. The annex contains the original version of the tool, used as the basis to develop the Polish version used in this research. Consequently, the items presented in the tables differ slightly from the original English version as a result of the back-translation procedure applied. The tool makes it possible to determine the degree of acceptance by individuals involved in the process of inclusive education, including teachers, of specific assumptions related to the organisation and implementation of this form of education. It consists of 60 items and includes seven subscales: Pedagogy for all learners, Support for learning, Leadership role and approaches, Learner well-being and participation, Curriculum development, Partnerships and collaborative working, and Support systems for staff and leaders. Cronbach's alpha reliability coefficients for these individual subscales range from 0.71 to 0.88 (determined using the 2020 and 2022 data).

An additional tool used to collect sociodemographic data and data related to the teaching profession was a survey questionnaire which included questions concerning gender, place of residence (urban/rural area), the type of facility where the respondent was employed (state, non-state) and the level taught (preschool, primary school levels 1 to 3, levels 4 to 8, or all primary school levels, secondary school), as well as job seniority and length of service at the current place of employment.

Description of the study group

A total of 6,042 teachers participated in the surveys. In 2020, the number of teachers surveyed was 3,189 vs 2,853 in 2022. The vast majority of the survey respondents were female teachers (5,090, i.e. 84.24%, while the number of male teachers was 952, i.e. 15.76%). A similar gender distribution characterised both groups of teachers: those surveyed in 2020 and those surveyed in 2022 (Table 3).

Table 3. Gender of the teachers surveyed in 2020 and 2022

Gender	Teachers surveyed in 2020		Teachers surveyed in 2022		Total	
	N	%	N	%	N	%
Women	2,615	82.00	2,475	86.8	5,090	84.24
Men	574	18.00	378	13.2	952	15.76
Total	3,189	100	2,853	100	6,042	100

The mean age of the teachers surveyed was M=50.53 (SD=7.93). In the group of teachers surveyed in 2020: M=50.70, SD=7.90, whereas in the group of teachers surveyed in 2022: M=50.35, SD=7.96. Most of the teachers surveyed were urban residents (3,794, i. e. 62.79%), while the number of teachers living in rural areas was 2,248, i. e. 37.21%). Data on the place of residence of the teachers surveyed in the two respective time periods is presented in Table 4.

Table 4. Place of residence of the teachers surveyed in 2020 and 2022

Place of residence	Teachers surveyed in 2020		Teachers surveyed in 2022		Total	
	N	%	N	%	N	%
Urban	1,992	62.5	1,802	63.2	3,794	62.79
Rural	1,197	37.5	1,051	36.8	2,248	37.21
Total	3,189	100	2,853	100	6,042	100

Mean job seniority among the teachers surveyed was M=27.93 (SD=41.41); among teachers surveyed in 2020: M=28.66 (SD=45.02), and among those surveyed in 2022: M=27.32 (SD=42.81). In turn, mean length of service at the current school was M=18.72 (SD=27.95); among the teachers surveyed in 2020: M=18.71 (SD=19.00), and among those surveyed in 2022: M=18.75 (SD=11.13). Most of the teachers surveyed were employed at state schools (4,320, i. e. 71.5%), and the number of teachers employed at non-state schools was 1,722 (28.5%) (Table 5).

Table 5. Type of school employing the teachers surveyed in 2020 and 2022

School type	Teachers surveyed in 2020		Teachers surveyed in 2022		Total	
	N	%	N	%	N	%
State	2,270	71.18	2,050	71.85	4,320	71.5
Non-state	919	28.82	803	28.15	1,722	28.5
Total	3,189	100	2,853	100	6,042	100

A comparable number of the teachers surveyed were employed at the different levels of education: pre-school, primary school levels 1 to 3, primary school levels 4 to 8, all primary school levels, and secondary school. The respective data are summarised in Table 6.

Table 6. Level taught by the teachers surveyed in 2020 and 2022

Level taught	Teachers surveyed in 2020		Teachers surveyed in 2022		Total	
	N	%	N	%	N	%
Pre-school	704	22.08	555	19.45	1,259	20.84
Primary school levels 1 to 3	605	18.97	570	19.98	1,175	19.45

Table 6 *(Continued)*

Level taught	Teachers surveyed in 2020		Teachers surveyed in 2022		Total	
	N	%	N	%	N	%
Primary school levels 4 to 8	617	19.35	568	19.91	1,185	19.61
Primary school (all levels)	672	21.07	590	20.68	1,262	20.88
Secondary school	591	18.53	570	19.98	1,161	19.22
Total	3,189	100	2,853	100	6,042	100

Chapter 4.
Teachers' beliefs about the validity of education for all

Validity of education for all – comparative analysis of 2020 and 2022 study results

The starting point adopted for the diagnosis of the opinions of teachers surveyed on various aspects of inclusive education was an analysis of the general beliefs concerning the validity of the existence and organisation of this type of education. It was assumed that the belief in the validity of education for all not only formed the basis underlying the development of teachers' attitudes towards other, more specific elements of inclusive education, but also reflected their concept/vision of education in general, in the context of the diverse needs and capabilities learners have. These beliefs become all the more relevant when the natural diversity of learners is joined by a high percentage of learners who are different due to being refugees, defined in a broad sense. Consequently, we analysed in the first place the beliefs concerning inclusive education in two groups of teachers, surveyed in two separate time frames, to reflect the key element differentiating Polish schools, namely the percentage of learners being war refugees from Ukraine. In their beliefs, the teachers referred to the validity of education for all, considering the diverse needs and capabilities, also in the context of inclusion of Ukrainian learners. We analysed these beliefs taking into account selected sociodemographic variables: gender, age and place of residence, as well as factors related to occupation and employment: job seniority, length of service at the current school, type of school where the teacher was employed, and the level of education taught.

Table 7. Beliefs of the teachers surveyed in 2020 and 2022 about the validity of education for all

Teachers' beliefs	Teachers surveyed in 2020		Teachers surveyed in 2022		df	t-test	p	Cohen's d
	M	SD	M	SD				
Generalised belief								
Education for all	51.27	5.00	49.54	5.72	6,040	12.52	<0.001	0.575
Specific beliefs								
Teachers are responsible for the learning/teaching of all learners in the classroom	4.63	0.55	4.50	0.69	6,040	8.22	<0.001	0.591
Teachers take steps to address the differentiated/diverse needs of all learners in the classroom	4.54	0.57	4.42	0.65	6,040	7.53	<0.001	0.559
Teachers are guided by sensitivity and respect towards learners	4.64	0.52	4.53	0.59	6,040	7.34	<0.001	0.548
Teachers have high expectations of all learners	3.79	0.88	3.53	0.96	6,040	11.04	<0.001	0.652
Teachers use evidence of scientifically proven effectiveness in making decisions concerning innovative approaches to learning	3.89	0.87	3.79	0.95	6,040	5.50	<0.001	0.455
Teachers help learners to reflect on their learning process and learning strategies	4.16	0.62	4.01	0.71	6,040	9.14	<0.001	0.823
Teachers personalise the learning process for all learners	4.18	0.66	3.97	0.77	6,040	11.52	<0.001	0.984
Teachers use flexible group-work formats (e.g., whole classroom, small groups, pairs) to enable learners to work together and have access to multiple points of view	4.42	0.57	4.29	0.66	6,040	8.42	<0.001	0.604
Teachers use diversified teaching aids and technologies to enhance the quality of learning	4.42	0.56	4.37	0.64	6,040	3.68	<0.001	0.400
Teachers offer learners diversified ways of demonstrating the knowledge and skills they should master	4.34	0.57	4.23	0.64	6,040	8.91	<0.001	0.879
Teachers use formative assessment, enabling learners to plan their next steps in the learning process	4.00	0.72	3.85	0.83	6,040	7.54	<0.001	0.831

Table 7 *(Continued)*

Teachers' beliefs	Teachers surveyed in 2020		Teachers surveyed in 2022		df	t-test	p	Cohen's d
	M	SD	M	SD				
Teachers provide feedback to learners focusing on their effort and progress	4.24	0.62	4.05	0.71	6,040	11.16	<0.001	0.940

M – arithmetic mean; SD – standard deviation; t – Student's t-test for independent data

The results of the analyses in Table 7 show statistically significant differences in the beliefs of the two groups of teachers surveyed concerning the validity of education for all. The teachers surveyed in 2020 scored significantly higher, both in the generalised belief in the validity of education for all, taking into account the learners' individual needs and capabilities. The beliefs of the teachers surveyed in 2022 are significantly weaker in this respect. The significant diversity identified between the two groups of teachers in this generalised belief is reflected in the significant differences in the specific beliefs, indicating that teachers have a key contribution both to the adequate understanding of inclusive education as well as to its proper organisation. However, it is important to emphasise that a large effect size of the identified difference was found in the case of some teachers' beliefs. These beliefs include the following: *Teachers personalise the learning process for all learners; Teachers provide feedback to learners focusing on their effort and progress; Teachers offer learners diversified ways of demonstrating the knowledge and skills they should master; Teachers use formative assessment, enabling learners to plan their next steps in the learning process;* and *Teachers help learners to reflect on their learning process and learning strategies.* The teachers surveyed in 2020 expressed a significantly stronger belief about the teacher's participation and role in inclusive education compared to the teachers surveyed in 2022.

Beliefs of the teachers surveyed in 2020 – importance of sociodemographic as well as job- and employment-specific variables

An analysis of the beliefs of the teachers surveyed in 2020 concerning the validity of education for all revealed that they might vary depending on certain sociodemographic as well as occupation- and employment-specific variables. The results obtained regarding the differentiating role of the respondents' gender are shown in Table 8. They indicate that female teachers have significantly stronger generalised beliefs in the analysed area compared to male teachers.

Table 8. Impact of gender on the beliefs of the teachers surveyed in 2020 about the validity of education for all

Teachers' beliefs	Female teachers		Male teachers		df	U-test	p
	M	SD	M	SD			
Generalised belief							
Education for all	51.34	5.00	49.90	4.97	3,186	1.89	0.049
Specific beliefs							
Teachers are responsible for the learning/teaching of all learners in the classroom	4.64	0.55	4.59	0.56	3,188	1.76	0.078
Teachers take steps to address the differentiated/diverse needs of all learners in the classroom	4.56	0.57	4.35	0.56	3,188	4.15	<0.001
Teachers are guided by sensitivity and respect towards learners	4.65	0.53	4.59	0.51	3,188	2.51	0.012
Teachers have high expectations of all learners	3.76	0.89	3.91	0.77	3,188	-3.68	<0.001
Teachers use evidence of scientifically proven effectiveness in making decisions concerning innovative approaches to learning	3.89	0.68	3.79	0.67	3,188	0.59	0.552
Teachers help learners to reflect on their learning process and learning strategies	4.16	0.62	4.20	0.60	3,188	-1.33	0.182
Teachers personalise the learning process for all learners	4.20	0.59	4.13	0.61	3,188	2.34	0.019
Teachers use flexible group-work formats (e.g., whole classroom, small groups, pairs) to enable learners to work together and have access to multiple points of view	4.45	0.55	4.31	0.52	3,188	5.43	<0.001
Teachers use diversified teaching aids and technologies to enhance the quality of learning	4.43	0.59	4.39	0.54	3,188	5.46	0.068
Teachers offer learners diversified ways of demonstrating the knowledge and skills they should master	4.35	0.55	4.29	0.57	3,188	1.82	0.034

Table 8 (Continued)

Teachers' beliefs	Female teachers		Male teachers		df	U-test	p
	M	SD	M	SD			
Teachers use formative assessment, enabling learners to plan their next steps in the learning process	4.01	0.61	3.92	0.58	3,188	1.13	0.126
Teachers provide feedback to learners focusing on their effort and progress	4.24	0.67	4.20	0.56	3,188	2.45	0.108

M – arithmetic mean; SD – standard deviation; U – Mann-Whitney U-test

The gender of the teachers surveyed in 2020 was found to be a differentiating factor for some of the specific beliefs about the validity of inclusive education. Female teachers scored significantly higher on the following beliefs: *Teachers take steps to address the differentiated/diverse needs of all learners in the classroom; Teachers are guided by sensitivity and respect towards learners; Teachers personalise the learning process for all learners; Teachers use flexible group-work formats (e.g., whole classroom, small groups, pairs) to enable learners to work together and have access to multiple points of view; Teachers offer learners diversified ways of demonstrating the knowledge and skills they should master*. Male teachers, on the other hand, scored significantly higher on the belief that *Teachers have high expectations of all learners*.

Further analyses examined the links between teachers' age and their beliefs about the validity of inclusive education. The Pearson's r correlation coefficient that was calculated revealed a negative relationship ($r=-0.471$, $p<0.001$). This means that the stronger beliefs of teachers in terms of the validity of inclusive education in the analysed area are associated with their younger age. The significance of another sociodemographic variable, namely place of residence, was also tested, indicating statistically significant differences in the beliefs of teachers living in urban and rural areas concerning the validity of inclusive education. The results are shown in Table 9.

The teachers surveyed in 2020 living in urban areas were characterised by a significantly stronger generalised belief in the validity of inclusive education compared to teachers living in rural areas. However, the effect size of the difference found was small. Significantly stronger beliefs were also revealed in the case of teachers from urban areas concerning the following matters: *Teachers are guided by sensitivity and respect towards learners; Teachers use evidence of scientifically proven effectiveness in making decisions concerning innovative approaches to learning; Teachers use diversified teaching aids and technologies to enhance the quality of learning;* and *Teachers offer learners diversified ways of demonstrating the knowledge and skills they should master*. It should be nevertheless noted at this point that the differences found, although statistically significant, have a low effect size.

In line with the assumptions, the role of occupation- and employment-specific variables was also tested with regard to the beliefs expressed by the teachers. Neither seniority nor length of service at the current school correlated significantly with beliefs about the validity of inclusive education for all learners ($r=-0.091$, $p=0.879$; $r=-0.111$, $p=0.598$, respectively). In contrast, the type of institution where the teacher was employed and the level of education taught significantly differentiated the teachers' beliefs analysed here. The results of analyses obtained in this area are presented in Tables 10 and 11.

Table 9. Impact of the place of residence on the beliefs of the teachers surveyed in 2020 about the validity of education for all

Teachers' beliefs	Urban teachers		Rural teachers		df	t-test	p	Cohen's d
	M	SD	M	SD				
Generalised belief								
Education for all	51.41	5.09	50.32	4.84	3,186	2.04	0.041	0.345
Specific beliefs								
Teachers are responsible for the learning/teaching of all learners in the classroom	4.63	0.55	4.62	0.53	3,186	0.32	0.751	-
Teachers take steps to address the differentiated/diverse needs of all learners in the classroom	4.54	0.55	4.52	0.58	3,186	1.04	0.300	-
Teachers are guided by sensitivity and respect towards learners	4.66	0.51	4.58	0.55	3,186	2.16	0.031	0.363
Teachers have high expectations of all learners	3.80	0.86	3.77	0.89	3,186	0.89	0.369	-
Teachers use evidence of scientifically proven effectiveness in making decisions concerning innovative approaches to learning	3.91	0.69	3.85	0.66	3,186	2.48	0.013	0.293
Teachers help learners to reflect on their learning process and learning strategies	4.16	0.65	4.17	0.58	3,186	-0.11	0.916	-
Teachers personalise the learning process for all learners	4.20	0.63	4.17	0.55	3,186	1.23	0.219	-
Teachers use flexible group-work formats (e.g., whole classroom, small groups, pairs) to enable learners to work together and have access to multiple points of view	4.44	0.51	4.40	0.60	3,186	1.72	0.086	-
Teachers use diversified teaching aids and technologies to enhance the quality of learning	4.44	0.56	4.39	0.61	3,186	2.26	0.024	0.227
Teachers offer learners diversified ways of demonstrating the knowledge and skills they should master	4.37	0.49	4.27	0.67	3,186	2.95	0.003	0.454
Teachers use formative assessment, enabling learners to plan their next steps in the learning process	4.01	0.59	4.97	0.66	3,186	0.97	0.333	-

Table 9 (*Continued*)

Teachers' beliefs	Urban teachers		Rural teachers		df	t-test	p	Cohen's d
	M	SD	M	SD				
Teachers provide feedback to learners focusing on their effort and progress	4.24	0.64	4.23	0.58	3,186	0.64	0.325	-

M – arithmetic mean; SD – standard deviation; t – Student's t-test for independent data

Table 10. Impact of the school type (state, non-state) on the beliefs of the teachers surveyed in 2020 about the validity of education for all

Teachers' beliefs	State school teachers		Non-state school teachers		df	U-test	p
	M	SD	M	SD			
Generalised belief							
Education for all	51.17	4.99	52.07	4.94	3,186	2.84	0.007
Specific beliefs							
Teachers are responsible for the learning/teaching of all learners in the classroom	4.63	0.55	4.60	0.57	3,186	1.06	0.289
Teachers take steps to address the differentiated/diverse needs of all learners in the classroom	4.53	0.58	4.59	0.51	3,186	-1.84	0.066
Teachers are guided by sensitivity and respect towards learners	4.63	0.53	4.69	0.46	3,186	-1.72	0.856
Teachers have high expectations of all learners	3.79	0.86	3.77	0.96	3,186	0.32	0.747
Teachers use evidence of scientifically proven effectiveness in making decisions concerning innovative approaches to learning	3.89	0.68	3.94	0.71	3,186	-1.38	0.167
Teachers help learners to reflect on their learning process and learning strategies	4.15	0.63	4.26	0.57	3,186	-2.93	0.003
Teachers personalise the learning process for all learners	4.17	0.54	4.33	0.57	3,186	-4.23	<0.001
Teachers use flexible group-work formats (e.g., whole classroom, small groups, pairs) to enable learners to work together and have access to multiple points of view	4.41	0.51	4.50	0.54	3,186	-2.57	0.010
Teachers use diversified teaching aids and technologies to enhance the quality of learning	4.42	0.65	4.49	0.67	3,186	-2.27	0.024
Teachers offer learners diversified ways of demonstrating the knowledge and skills they should master	4.33	0.71	4.44	0.68	3,186	-3.11	0.002
Teachers use formative assessment, enabling learners to plan their next steps in the learning process	3.99	0.59	4.12	0.62	3,186	-2.99	0.002
Teachers provide feedback to learners focusing on their effort and progress	4.23	0.62	4.34	0.59	3,186	-3.02	0.003

M – arithmetic mean; SD – standard deviation; U – Mann-Whitney U-test

The analysis showed that teachers from non-state schools were characterised by significantly stronger generalised beliefs about the validity of inclusive education for all compared to teachers working in state schools. Significant differences between these groups of teachers were also found within the area of specific beliefs. Teachers from non-state schools express the following beliefs significantly more often: *Teachers help learners to reflect on their learning process and learning strategies; Teachers personalise the learning process for all learners; Teachers use flexible group-work formats (e. g., whole classroom, small groups, pairs) to enable learners to work together and have access to multiple points of view; Teachers use diversified teaching aids and technologies to enhance the quality of learning; Teachers offer learners diversified ways of demonstrating the knowledge and skills they should master; Teachers use formative assessment, enabling learners to plan their next steps in the learning process;* and *Teachers provide feedback to learners focusing on their effort and progress.* Thus, teachers from non-state schools are much more convinced that the role of teachers in education for all manifests itself in developing and strengthening a vision of learning together, individualising the teaching process, and organising the educational process in such a way as to serve all learners and ensure progress in their development.

Teachers employed at different levels of education (pre-school, primary school levels 1 to 3, primary school levels 4 to 8, all primary school levels, secondary schools) differ statistically significantly in terms of their expressed beliefs concerning the validity of inclusive education for all. Significant differences were found both in generalised beliefs and in almost all specific beliefs concerning the various elements of teachers' contribution to the shaping of views and to organising inclusive education for all learners. Pre-school education teachers expressed the strongest beliefs, differing significantly in this respect from secondary and primary school teachers (those working at levels 4 to 8 and at all levels).

The level of education taught differentiated significantly almost all specific beliefs, with the pre-school teacher group differing significantly in most of the beliefs expressed in terms of the intensity of beliefs concerning the individual planes of participation of teachers in education for all learners. Only with regard to the belief *Teachers have high expectations of all learners* were there no statistically significant differences between the teacher groups surveyed.

Table 11. Impact of the level taught on the beliefs of the teachers surveyed in 2020 on the validity of education for all

Beliefs	Pre-school teachers (1)		Teachers of primary school levels 1 to 3 (2)		Teachers of primary school levels 4 to 8 (3)		Teachers of all primary school levels (4)		Secondary school teachers (5)		One-way ANOVA		
	M	SD	M	SD	M	SD	M	SD	M	SD	F	Inter-group comparison	p
Generalised belief													
Education for all	52.11	4.85	51.46	5.03	50.98	4.95	50.74	5.10	51.27	4.99	12.39***	1–3 1–4 1–5	0.016 0.004 0.019
Specific beliefs													
1	4.67	0.50	4.62	0.59	4.65	0.46	4.64	0.55	4.56	0.60	3.84**	1–5 4–5	<0.001 0.004
2	4.63	0.53	4.56	0.63	4.75	0.46	4.52	0.58	4.45	0.57	10.73***	1–4 1–5 2–5 4–5	<0.001 <0.001 0.004 0.012
3	4.74	0.47	4.65	0.52	4.74	0.46	4.61	0.55	4.57	0.53	13.03***	1–2 1–4 1–5 2–5	0.046 0.022 0.027 0.033
4	3.79	0.91	3.79	0.89	3.38	0.92	3.78	0.81	3.80	0.67	0.50	–	
5	4.00	0.67	3.88	0.68	3.99	0.75	3.83	0.68	3.89	0.69	6.90***	1–2 1–4 1–5	0.032 <0.001 0.001
6	4.14	0.66	4.15	0.59	4.13	0.84	4.16	0.61	4.21	0.59	7.87***	1–5 3–5	0.020 0.041

Table 11 (Continued)

Beliefs	Pre-school teachers (1)		Teachers of primary school levels 1 to 3 (2)		Teachers of primary school levels 4 to 8 (3)		Teachers of all primary school levels (4)		Secondary school teachers (5)		One-way ANOVA		
	M	SD	M	SD	M	SD	M	SD	M	SD	F	Inter-group comparison	p
7	4.28	0.66	4.16	0.65	4.38	0.52	4.17	0.64	4.11	0.58	4.53**	1–2 1–4 1–5 4–5	0.025 <0.001 <0.001 0.039
8	4.53	0.55	4.42	0.56	4.75	0.46	4.39	0.56	4.36	0.57	6.90***	1–2 1–4 1–5	0.019 <0.001 <0.001
9	4.51	0.56	4.42	0.53	4.63	0.52	4.41	0.55	4.36	0.49	11.16***	1–2 1–4 1–5	0.047 <0.001 <0.001
10	4.42	0.60	4.39	0.52	4.62	0.54	4.31	0.57	4.32	0.56	7.82***	1–4 1–5	<0.001 0.001
11	4.10	0.58	4.12	0.56	4.25	0.51	3.97	0.55	3.91	0.57	6.18***	1–4 1–5 2–4 2–5	<0.001 0.001 0.008 <0.001

Table 11 (Continued)

Beliefs	Pre-school teachers (1)		Teachers of primary school levels 1 to 3 (2)		Teachers of primary school levels 4 to 8 (3)		Teachers of all primary school levels (4)		Secondary school teachers (5)		One-way ANOVA		
	M	SD	M	SD	M	SD	M	SD	M	SD	F	Inter-group comparison	p
12	4.30	0.65	4.30	0.54	4.75	0.65	4.21	0.59	4.20	0.62	5.49**	1–3	0.041
												1–4	0.001
												1–5	0.001
												2–3	0.042
												2–5	0.049
												3–4	0.014
												3–5	0.012

1: Teachers are responsible for the learning/teaching of all learners in the classroom; 2: Teachers take steps to address the differentiated/diverse needs of all learners in the classroom; 3: Teachers are guided by sensitivity and respect towards learners; 4: Teachers have high expectations of all learners; 5: Teachers use evidence of scientifically proven effectiveness in making decisions concerning innovative approaches to learning; 6: Teachers help learners to reflect on their learning process and learning strategies; 7: Teachers personalise the learning process for all learners; 8: Teachers use flexible group-work formats (e.g., whole classroom, small groups, pairs) to enable learners to work together and have access to multiple points of view; 9: Teachers use diversified teaching aids and technologies to enhance the quality of learning; 10: Teachers offer learners diversified ways of demonstrating the knowledge and skills they should master; 11: Teachers use formative assessment, enabling learners to plan their next steps in the learning process; 12: Teachers provide feedback to learners focusing on their effort and progress

In terms of the teachers' responsibility for teaching all learners in the classroom, pre-school teachers expressed the strongest opinion, significantly stronger than that of secondary school teachers, who also scored significantly lower in this regard compared to primary school teachers. Pre-school teachers were also statistically significantly different from primary and secondary school teachers in terms of manifesting stronger beliefs with regard to teachers taking initiatives to address the different needs of all learners in the classroom. It is worth noting that secondary school teachers expressed the weakest beliefs in this respect, scoring significantly lower than primary school levels 1 to 3 teachers and those employed at all levels of primary education. In its essence, inclusive education assumes respect towards each learner and the qualities they possess. This belief was confirmed to the highest degree by pre-school teachers, differing significantly from primary school levels 1 to 3 teachers, those employed at primary schools in general, and secondary school teachers. The latter scored lowest on this belief, additionally demonstrating significant diversity compared to primary school levels 1 to 3 teachers. Pre-school teachers also believed most strongly that the teacher's role in inclusive education would involve taking into account scientific developments pointing to the effectiveness of certain innovative methods of working with learners, applicable in the teaching process. This is furthermore linked to using of flexible forms of work with the group, leading to interactions between all learners, as well as to implementing a variety of teaching aids to systematically improve the quality of learning for learners with individual needs. With regard to the aforementioned beliefs, this group of teachers was statistically significantly different from primary school levels 1 to 3, other primary school levels and secondary schools teachers. The same result was obtained in their case for the belief that teachers personalise the learning process for all learners. Compared to primary and secondary school teachers, pre-school teachers revealed significantly stronger beliefs concerning teachers offering learners a variety of ways of demonstrating their knowledge and skills, teachers' use of assessment enabling learners to plan their next steps in learning, and teachers' feedback given to learners on their effort and progress.

Importantly, secondary school teachers scored highest only on the belief *Teachers help learners to reflect on their learning process and learning strategies*, differing significantly in this respect from pre-school and level 4 to 8 teachers. It is worth noting at this point that the greatest diversity between the groups of teachers surveyed was found with regard to the belief concerning teachers providing feedback to learners on their progress and effort. The highest score here was obtained by teachers of levels 4 to 8, differing statistically significantly from all the other groups of teachers surveyed (pre-school, primary school levels 1 to 3, primary school covering all levels, and secondary schools).

Beliefs of the teachers surveyed in 2022 – importance of sociodemographic as well as job- and employment-specific variables

Similarly to the group of teachers surveyed in 2020, we analysed beliefs concerning the validity of inclusive education for all learners among the teachers surveyed in 2022. The analyses also took into account sociodemographic variables: gender, age and place of residence, as well as variables related to the occupation and employment of the teachers surveyed (seniority, length of service at the current school, type of school and level of education taught). The results obtained in this group of teachers, within the analyses covering the individual factors, point to slightly different interpretative trends, compared to the findings among the teachers surveyed in 2020.

An analysis of the influence of gender on the strength of beliefs of the teachers surveyed in 2022 concerning the validity of education for all revealed that female and male teachers did not differ statistically significantly in this respect ($M_{female\ teachers}$=49.58; SD=5.72; $M_{male\ teachers}$=49.23; SD=5.70; Mann-Whitney U=0.65; p=0.513). The age of the teachers surveyed did not reveal any significant associations with their beliefs about the validity of inclusive education for all (r= -0.091; p=760). The third sociodemographic variable adopted, i. e. place of residence, did not significantly differentiate the teachers' beliefs analysed here either. Teachers living in urban and rural areas indicated similar beliefs (lower, however, than the teachers surveyed in 2020): $M_{urban\ teachers}$=49.56; SD=5.86; $M_{rural\ teachers}$=49.51; SD=5.47; t=1.21; p=0.830.

Different results, compared to those obtained in the group of teachers surveyed in 2020, were obtained among the teachers surveyed in 2022 as part of the testing of the links between seniority/length of service at the current place of employment and beliefs expressed about the validity of inclusive education for all. Stronger beliefs of this type among teachers are associated with their longer seniority, whereas the positive correlation found between these variables was found to be weak (r=0.392; p=0.01). Working longer at the current place of employment was associated with higher scores within the analysed beliefs in this group of teachers (r=0.451; p=0.001). The relationship between the variables found here, although statistically significant, also turned out to be relatively weak.

In contrast to the results of the teachers surveyed in 2020, another differentiating variable analysed, i. e. the type of school, did not prove to be significant for the beliefs expressed about the validity of inclusive education for all learners in the teachers surveyed in 2022. Teachers employed at state schools and teachers working at non-state schools obtained similar results in this respect ($M_{state\ school}$

$_{\text{teachers}}$=49.53; SD=5.68; $M_{\text{non-state school teachers}}$=49.82; SD=6.57; Mann-Whitney U=2.23; p=0.892).

In turn, statistically significant diversity was recorded in the beliefs of the teachers surveyed in 2022 taking into account the level of education taught. The results obtained in this respect are presented in Table 10.

In terms of the generalised belief about the validity of education for all, secondary school teachers scored lowest, significantly lower than the other respondent groups. Teachers employed at different education levels display significantly different strength of specific beliefs relating to the specified levels of teachers' involvement in shaping and developing inclusive education for all learners. It is important to emphasise that no statistically significant differences were found between the different groups of teachers with regard to five beliefs. The findings obtained in 2022, convergent with the ones obtained for the teachers surveyed in 2020, indicate that pre-school teachers display by far the strongest specific beliefs.

An analysis of the individual beliefs yielded the following results. Regarding the question of teachers' responsibility for teaching all learners in the classroom, secondary school teachers scored the lowest, differing statistically significantly in this respect from the other groups of teachers surveyed. The belief concerning the initiative taken by teachers in addressing the diverse needs of all learners in the classroom was expressed most strongly by pre-school teachers, compared to teachers of levels 4 to 8 in primary schools and secondary school teachers. The latter group also differed significantly in this belief from primary school levels 1 to 3 teachers and teachers at primary school covering all levels. Characteristically, secondary school teachers score the lowest on the belief that teachers are guided by sensitivity and respect for learners, differing significantly in this respect from pre-school, primary school levels 1 to 3 teachers, and other primary school teachers. The use of scientific evidence in the selection of innovative approaches to learning is the belief expressed most strongly by pre-school teachers, significantly more strongly compared to teachers of primary school levels 4 to 8, teachers at all primary school levels, and secondary school teachers. With regard to the use of flexible forms of group work, ensuring that learners work together and that multiple points of view are taken into account, secondary school teachers were the least convinced, differing in this respect from pre-school and primary school levels 1 to 3 teachers, as well as teachers at primary schools covering all levels. The greatest diversity between the teacher groups surveyed was found with regard to the following beliefs: *Teachers personalise the learning process for all learners* and *Teachers use formative assessment, enabling learners to plan their next steps in the learning process.* Within both these beliefs, secondary school teachers scored the lowest, significantly lower than all the other teacher groups.

Table 12. Impact of the level taught on the beliefs of the teachers surveyed in 2022 about the validity of education for all

Beliefs	Pre-school teachers (1)		Teachers of primary school levels 1 to 3 (2)		Teachers of primary school levels 4 to 8 (3)		Teachers of all primary school levels (4)		Secondary school teachers (5)		One-way ANOVA		
	M	SD	M	SD	M	SD	M	SD	M	SD	F	Inter-group comparison	p
Generalised belief													
Education for all	50.09	5.87	49.65	5.63	49.53	5.41	49.69	5.78	48.15	5.72	3.80**	1–5 2–5 3–5 4–5	0.001 0.010 0.026 0.003
Specific beliefs													
1	4.45	0.59	4.49	0.67	4.48	0.68	4.56	0.65	4.39	0.83	6.24***	1–5 2–5 3–5 4–5	<0.001 0.008 0.022 <0.001
2	4.48	0.61	4.44	0.62	4.39	0.64	4.45	0.65	4.32	0.73	4.62***	1–3 1–5 2–5 4–5	0.036 <0.001 0.006 0.001
3	4.55	0.59	4.54	0.60	4.51	0.58	4.58	0.56	4.46	0.59	3.95**	1–5 2–5 3–4 4–5	0.013 0.030 0.024 <0.001
4	3.57	0.98	3.47	0.96	3.52	0.97	3.56	0.95	3.50	0.96	1.20	–	

Table 12 (Continued)

Beliefs	Pre-school teachers (1)		Teachers of primary school levels 1 to 3 (2)		Teachers of primary school levels 4 to 8 (3)		Teachers of all primary school levels (4)		Secondary school teachers (5)		One-way ANOVA		
	M	SD	M	SD	M	SD	M	SD	M	SD	F	Inter-group comparison	p
5	3.99	0.76	3.81	0.71	3.77	0.71	3.77	0.73	3.75	0.74	3.03*	1-3 1-4 1-5	0.010 0.003 0.002
6	3.94	0.81	4.04	0.69	4.02	0.68	4.03	0.69	3.99	0.71	1.80	-	
7	4.07	0.75	3.97	0.78	4.01	0.71	3.98	0.74	3.85	0.83	5.58***	1-2 1-5 2-5 3-5 4-5	0.043 <0.001 0.013 0.001 0.002
8	4.35	0.68	4.30	0.66	4.28	0.64	4.31	0.64	4.20	0.71	3.74**	1-5 2-5 4-5	<0.001 0.011 0.003
9	4.39	0.66	4.39	0.64	4.37	0.65	4.35	0.64	4.34	0.61	0.73	-	
10	4.22	0.67	4.27	0.65	4.25	0.63	4.22	0.64	4.21	0.65	0.75	-	
11	3.94	0.71	3.87	0.80	3.99	0.81	3.84	0.84	3.74	0.86	3.93**	1-4 1-5 2-5 3-5 4-5	0.047 <0.001 0.012 0.005 0.028

Table 12 *(Continued)*

Beliefs	Pre-school teachers (1)		Teachers of primary school levels 1 to 3 (2)		Teachers of primary school levels 4 to 8 (3)		Teachers of all primary school levels (4)		Secondary school teachers (5)		One-way ANOVA		
	M	SD	M	SD	M	SD	M	SD	M	SD	F	Inter-group comparison	p
12	4.12	0.69	4.06	0.71	4.04	0.73	4.03	0.71	4.00	0.72	1.92	-	

1: Teachers are responsible for the learning/teaching of all learners in the classroom; 2: Teachers take steps to address the differentiated/diverse needs of all learners in the classroom; 3: Teachers are guided by sensitivity and respect towards learners; 4: Teachers have high expectations of all learners; 5: Teachers use evidence of scientifically proven effectiveness in making decisions concerning innovative approaches to learning; 6: Teachers help learners to reflect on their learning process and learning strategies; 7: Teachers personalise the learning process for all learners; 8: Teachers use flexible group-work formats (e.g., whole classroom, small groups, pairs) to enable learners to work together and have access to multiple points of view; 9: Teachers use diversified teaching aids and technologies to enhance the quality of learning; 10: Teachers offer learners diversified ways of demonstrating the knowledge and skills they should master; 11: Teachers use formative assessment, enabling learners to plan their next steps in the learning process; 12: Teachers provide feedback to learners focusing on their effort and progress

Conclusion and discussion

Summarising the analyses performed concerning teachers' beliefs about the validity of inclusive education for all, we can point to the prominent role of certain factors that reveal the complex context in which their approach was formed. The measurement of beliefs in two time frames showed that teachers in 2020 were significantly more convinced of the rightness of organising and implementing inclusive education compared to teachers in 2022. They saw their own role in this process as more important, especially with regard to the possibility of personalising teaching taking into account learners' diverse needs, providing feedback to learners on their progress, systematically varying working methods, and maintaining a relationship with the learner in terms of establishing learning strategies, as well as setting the assessment of teaching outcomes in such a way as to enable creative planning of the subsequent stages of education. The change in such beliefs that was captured, not only on the level of statistical significance, but also with regard to the high effect size recorded, makes it possible to assume that a genuine transformation has taken place in the opinion of Polish school teachers on the validity of inclusive education. As a result, it also suggests the need to seek potential sources, making it possible not only to explain this phenomenon, but also to offer some practical recommendations, e. g. on how to disseminate constructive and realistic information about inclusive education for all.

In terms of strengthening inclusive education and building quality education for all learners in mainstream institutions, the changes shown should be considered unfavourable. When looking for the determinants of the change in teachers' attitudes over the period of two years, two factors are worth pointing out.

The first one involves the significant increase in the number of learners from Ukraine, already mentioned earlier, which has proven to pose a significant educational challenge for the system as a whole. The main burden brought about by this change has been felt by teachers. It is worth mentioning at this point that in the past, they were not prepared (or prepared to a small extent) to work with a culturally diverse group, especially with learners for whom Polish was a foreign language, although the presence of Ukrainian learners in Polish schools before 2022 had already been statistically noticeable (Syrnyk, 2017). On 8 April 2022, a relevant normative act was published on the presence of Ukrainian learners in Polish schools (*Regulation of the Minister of Education and Science of 8 April 2022*), but it left many practical problems unsolved. Arguably, teachers would be supported by manuals on working with Ukrainian learners (e.g., Rafał-Łuniewska, 2022), but research results show that this support has been insufficient. One of the first more extensive studies conducted after Russia's aggression against Ukraine in Polish schools (Pyżalski et al., 2022) on a group of 792 teachers (mainly in primary schools) showed that more than half of the respondents (56%) indicated a very high or high burden related to the assessment for Ukrainian children. A substantial group of respondents (55.8%) pointed to significant problems with setting educational goals for such learners, as it was difficult to determine how long they would stay at their Polish schools. In addition, the teachers surveyed indicated significant burdens related to the unfavourable regulations governing school attendance of these learners (38.9%), their high fluctuation (38.9%) – short stay and changing of residence, difficulties in communicating with them (37.5%), their poor commitment to learning (35.9%), differences in the standards and rules of upbringing of Polish and Ukrainian children (30.2%), and many other problems (Pyżalski et al., 2022, pp. 40–41).

Although the recent scale of war migration is unprecedented in the history of post-war Europe, it has lately been encountered elsewhere in the world too. For example, over the recent years, some four million people have had to migrate from Iraq and Syria to Turkey. According to research, Turkish school teachers have faced similar issues related to the reinforcing cultural diversity at school, as well as struggled with an unprepared system to accommodate so many learners arriving from abroad in a short period of time (Aydin & Kaya, 2019; Soylu, Kaysılı, & Sever, 2020). This is different compared to the situation seen in many countries (e. g., France, Germany, Sweden, and Denmark), where intercultural schools have been built systematically for many years now, with substantial funding allocated to a large extent to long-term teacher support. It should not be found surprising, therefore, that Polish school teachers have experienced a situation they were unprepared for, which resulted in turn in a feeling of being strongly burdened. As a result, they have changed their attitude towards inclusive education at least in part, by considering it a difficult project to implement – which explains the unfavourable change in the survey results in the second measurement.

The second factor that may have contributed to the change in attitude among the teachers surveyed, lowering their support for inclusive education, is related to the widespread media discussion on two drafts for reforming the Polish education system published by the then Ministry of National Education: *Model edukacji dla wszystkich* [*A Model of Education for All*] (2020) and *Wspieranie podnoszenia jakości edukacji włączającej w Polsce* [*Supporting the Improvement of Quality of Inclusive Education in Poland*] (2020).

Both drafts included a set of synchronised, systemic changes aimed at developing inclusive education. The draft reform model also envisaged changes in the scope of operation of facilities providing diagnosis and support to preschools and mainstream schools. Many of the proposed solutions raised not only concerns, but also strong controversy. In the media discourse, this was repeatedly boosted by fake news, for instance about the alleged plans to abolish special schools and to include all learners with disabilities in mainstream education (e. g., *Reforma edukacji włączającej...*, 2021; *MEiN planuje duże zmiany...* 2021). Furthermore, the draft was integrated into political debates and treated by far-right movements as an ideology aimed at destroying the Polish school (e. g., *Groźna iluzja inkluzji...*, 2022; *Manifest Komunistyczny edukacji włączającej*, 2022). As a result, the draft raised concerns among many teachers and reinforced negative or ambivalent attitudes towards inclusive education. The period from 2020 to 2022 was therefore not favourable for the promotion of inclusive education, which definitely contributed to the lower understanding of this form of teaching and education revealed in the results of the 2022 survey.

The selected sociodemographic as well as occupation- and employment-related factors that were taken into account revealed additional interpretative elements, significant in investigations aimed at gaining a better understanding of teachers' beliefs about the validity of education for all. Gender was found to differentiate these beliefs, but only among the teachers surveyed in 2020. In that study, female teachers expressed significantly stronger beliefs than male teachers, especially with regard to the teachers' specific activities aimed at organising and implementing inclusive education, e. g. their commitment to recognising learners' diverse needs in the learning process, showing respect and sensitivity towards each learner, striving to personalise methods of working with individual learners, and ensuring flexibility in this respect. It is worth emphasising at this point that male teachers underscored much more strongly the role of high expectations directed at all learners in inclusive education, compared to female teachers. These findings are in line with some studies showing more positive attitudes towards inclusive education among female teachers vs male teachers (Lindner, Schwab, Emara, & Avramidis, 2023). Having said that, it is important to note that broader meta-analyses of the relationship between teachers' gender and their attitudes towards the form of education discussed here do not show significant relationships (Orakci et al., 2016).

It is difficult to clearly explain the data presented in Table 8. In the case of the Polish education system, however, it is possible to put forward the proposition that male teachers are much more likely to work at the upper primary and secondary school levels than at pre-school and lower primary school levels. In Poland, training of subject teachers is very modest and usually takes place while pursuing the main curriculum of the relevant course (e. g., mathematics, physics, Polish, history, etc.), or is acquired during short postgraduate studies, strongly criticised by researchers studying teachers' competencies (Krause, Muchacka, & Przybyliński, 2017). In the process of acquiring subject teaching qualifications, most candidates acquire practically no competencies to work with a diverse group, do not learn about the methodology of special education and, as a result, are unprepared to work with learners with disabilities or learners coming from migrant and war refugee families (Bartnikowska & Wójcik, 2004; Chrzanowska, 2019a; Gajdzica, 2020). Pre-school and primary school levels 1 to 3 teacher candidates, on the other hand, undergo a thorough course in the field of special pedagogy. Consequently, the pedagogical and psychological preparation of those teaching at the first stages of education is much more thorough, and their attitude towards inclusive education is more positive (Chrzanowska, 2019).

Thus, as a result of this finding, distanced attitudes towards inclusive education among men are probably a consequence of the latter's statistically more frequent work at higher levels of education and their modest competencies in the field of special education acquired during their studies (including postgraduate courses).

Age was statistically significantly associated with the beliefs of teachers summarised here, but only in the case of those surveyed in 2020. Stronger beliefs in the validity of inclusive education were characteristic of teachers of a younger age. This relationship is confirmed by some research findings indicating a correlation between attitudes towards inclusive education and teachers' age (Hwang & Evans, 2011; Saloviita, 2020; Barnová et al., 2022), indicating more positive attitudes among younger teachers, although some data also confirms that longer seniority and the related experience foster positive attitudes towards inclusive education among older teachers (Lindner, Schwab, Emara, & Avramidis, 2023).

Significantly, another sociodemographic variable, i.e. place of residence, was also found to differentiate teachers' beliefs, but again only in the case of those surveyed in 2020. Urban teachers were more convinced of the validity of inclusive education for all learners, pointing to the importance of using scientific evidence in making decisions about the educational process, or of implementing teaching aids to improve the quality of education, as well as taking care to offer diversified ways of testing learners' knowledge and skills. These results may be surprising in view of the reports showing positive attitudes of rural teachers in other countries (Meng, 2008; McGhie-Richmond et al., 2013), as well as in Poland (Skotnicka, 2019). Nevertheless, barriers have also been reported to the inclusion of people with disabilities in rural areas (Marciniak-Madejska, 2014), as a consequence of the social attitudes of rural residents towards the needs of people with disabilities.

Interesting results were also recorded for the variables related to seniority. Teachers' beliefs about the validity of education for all were stronger among those working longer in the profession and at their current workplace, but only among those surveyed in 2022. At the same time, it is important to note that the correlation found was statistically significant, albeit weak. Whether a teacher was employed by a state or non-state school proved significant, but only among the group of teachers surveyed in 2020. Teachers from non-state schools expressed significantly stronger beliefs in the validity of inclusive education, which may be associated with a greater openness towards diversity and a general preference for more alternative forms of education (Kurniawati et al., 2012). Teachers in non-state schools emphasised much more strongly the teacher's role in organising this type of education, mainly in terms of its personalisation to meet the needs and capabilities of the learners, making working methods more flexible, determining specific learning strategies with all learners, using diversified teaching aids to enhance the quality of education, and providing constructive feedback to learners on their progress.

The level of education taught, in turn, differentiated teachers' beliefs significantly, both among the 2020 respondents and in the group surveyed in 2022. Some similar results can be indicated here. Pre-school teachers expressed the strongest beliefs about the validity of inclusive education, while secondary school teachers were the least convinced. These results can be explained by recalling the previously described process of acquiring teaching qualifications in Poland, which requires thorough teaching studies (including the completion of extensive special needs education modules) in the case of pre-school and primary school levels 1 to 3 teachers, and the possibility of acquiring full qualifications to teach subjects at higher levels without having to learn about the aspects related to acquiring competencies to work with a diverse group.

At the same time, it is worth noting that greater differences in the specific beliefs about inclusive education were found among the teachers surveyed in 2020. The group surveyed in 2022 agreed to a greater extent, regardless of the level of education taught, about the teacher's lesser role in inclusive education compared to the group surveyed in 2020.

Generalising on the basis of the analysis performed, it should be concluded that weaker beliefs about the validity of inclusive education among the teachers surveyed in 2022 were not differentiated by sociodemographic variables, i.e. gender, age, or place of residence. A factor providing some interpretative context is seniority: a shorter length of service was associated with weaker beliefs among teachers about the validity of inclusive education for all learners. The level of education taught may also be a certain point of reference. It was found to be significant for both groups of teachers, those surveyed in 2020 and those surveyed in 2022.

Chapter 5.
Learners' subjectivity in inclusive education as rated by teachers

Learners' subjectivity as rated by teachers – comparative analysis of 2020 and 2022 study results

Notable elements of inclusive education and its underlying premises include focusing on the well-being of each learner as well as highlighting and developing their potential, taking into account their traits, needs, and capabilities. The learner's well-being, placed in the broad category of their subjectivity, constitutes the essence of inclusive education, forming, as it were, the constitutive premise underlying any deliberations on the inclusive education of learners with diverse needs. The principles related to the remaining aspects of education for all are usually defined with reference to the well-being of each learner, recognising their uniqueness and specific conglomerate of traits. While the category of the child's well-being and subjectivity may be taken for granted, it is nevertheless not always fully realised in practice. In this research project, we analysed it in the context of its relevance to gain a full understanding of inclusive education. The analysis concerned the opinions of the teachers surveyed in 2020 and in 2022 on subjectivity in inclusive education, including the learners' well-being, taking into account the sociodemographic as well as job- and employment-related variables adopted. The findings indicate that the teachers surveyed in 2020 rated recognising learners' subjectivity in inclusive education significantly higher than the teachers surveyed in 2022 (Table 13). It is worth noting here that a medium effect size was found in the difference recorded. Furthermore, it is important to emphasise that significant differences were found between the two groups of teachers in terms of their rating of all specific aspects of learners' subjectivity in inclusive education. Nevertheless, the effect size recorded in them was low to medium.

Table 13. Recognising learners' subjectivity as rated by the teachers surveyed in 2020 and 2022

Teachers' rating	Teachers surveyed in 2020		Teachers surveyed in 2022		df	t-test	p	Cohen's d
	M	SD	M	SD				
Overall rating								
Learners' subjectivity	53.59	5.13	51.01	6.31	6,040	17.43	<0.001	0.730
Specific ratings								
All staff are responsible for the learners' well-being, seeing it as crucial to the learners' success	4.61	0.74	4.42	0.67	6,040	13.04	<0.001	0.297
All staff perceive learner diversity as an asset to the school	4.35	0.67	4.05	0.75	6,040	15.51	<0.001	0.469
School provides support to reduce any barriers to attendance (e.g., bullying, family situation)	4.56	0.78	4.38	0.80	6,040	11.78	<0.001	0.381
All staff support and encourage positive peer relationships	4.59	0.76	4.41	0.73	6,040	11.70	<0.001	0.372
The school climate enables learners to feel a sense of "belonging"	4.59	0.78	4.41	0.80	6,040	11.93	<0.001	0.374
The learners' voice is essential for the school community (daily action and directions for improvement)	4.25	0.60	3.98	0.62	6,040	15.72	<0.001	0.422
All staff encourage learners to see mistakes as learning opportunities	4.28	0.66	4.03	0.79	6,040	14.49	<0.001	0.391
All staff support learners to participate in learning activities to their full potential	4.46	0.59	4.21	0.62	6,040	16.00	<0.001	0.401
All staff encourage learners to be independent and responsible for themselves	4.48	0.76	4.26	0.78	6,040	13.59	<0.001	0.344
Procedures for dealing with discriminatory language and attitudes are always followed	4.32	0.67	4.09	0.70	6,040	12.55	<0.001	0.359
Conflicts/violent incidents are resolved promptly	4.62	0.80	4.42	0.83	6,040	12.74	<0.001	0.413
Learners can talk to school staff about personal problems that affect their learning	4.49	0.98	4.35	0.96	6,040	9.00	<0.001	4.290

M – arithmetic mean; SD – standard deviation; t – Student's t-test for independent data

In the subsequent part of the analyses, learners' subjectivity was compared in the context of sociodemographic as well as occupation- and employment-related variables, first among the teachers surveyed in 2020 and then among those surveyed in 2022.

Learners' subjectivity as rated by the teachers surveyed in 2020 – importance of sociodemographic as well as job- and employment-related variables

Firstly, we analysed the importance of gender in rating the recognition of learners' subjectivity in inclusive education in this group of teachers. Female teachers scored significantly higher than male teachers in this respect (Table 14). Statistically significant differences were also recorded in relation to the rating of almost all detailed aspects of subjectivity, except the rating concerning the prompt resolution of conflicts and acts of violence between learners, as well as the staff's perception of learner diversity as an asset to the school.

Correlational analysis showed that teachers' age was statistically significantly (albeit weakly) linked to their rating of learners' subjectivity. Younger teachers rated significantly higher the recognition of learners' subjectivity in inclusive education ($r=-0.18$, $p=0.034$). In turn, the place of residence of the teachers surveyed in 2020 did not significantly differentiate their rating with regard to recognising learners' subjectivity in inclusive education ($M_{urban\ teachers}=53.70$, $SD=5.21$, $M_{rural\ teachers}=53.40$, $SD=5.01$, $t=1.54$, $p=121$).

An analysis of the associations between occupation-related variables showed that seniority and length of service at the current school were not statistically significantly associated with the teachers' rating of the recognition of learners' subjectivity in inclusive education ($r=0.008$, $p=0.669$; $r=-0.023$, $p=0.193$, respectively). In turn, the type of school where the teachers taught proved to be a variable significantly differentiating their rating of the recognition of learners' subjectivity in inclusive education. The results obtained in this area are presented in Table 15. Teachers from non-state schools rated the recognition of learners' subjectivity in inclusive education significantly higher compared to state school teachers. Significantly higher ratings were also expressed by this group of teachers in relation to the following specific aspects of recognising this subjectivity: the staff's perception of learners' diversity as an asset to the school; the staff's encouragement of learners to treat mistakes as learning opportunities; the school's procedures for dealing with discriminatory language and attitudes being followed at all times; as well as learners being able to talk to school staff about personal problems affecting their learning process.

Table 14. Impact of teachers' gender on the rating of recognising learners' subjectivity among the teachers surveyed in 2020

Teachers' rating	Female teachers		Male teachers		df	U-test	p
	M	SD	M	SD			
Overall rating							
Learners' subjectivity	53.75	5.16	52.86	4.96	3,186	3.54	<0.001
Specific ratings							
All staff are responsible for the learners' well-being, seeing it as crucial to the learners' success	4.63	0.98	4.54	0.93	3,186	3.52	<0.001
All staff perceive learner diversity as an asset to the school	4.36	0.77	4.30	0.67	3,186	1.90	0.057
School provides support to reduce any barriers to attendance (e.g., bullying, family situation)	4.57	0.87	4.50	0.84	3,186	2.92	0.003
All staff support and encourage positive peer relationships	4.61	0.78	4.50	0.80	3,186	4.93	<0.001
The school climate enables learners to feel a sense of "belonging"	4.60	0.58	4.53	0.60	3,186	2.95	0.003
The learners' voice is essential for the school community (daily action and directions for improvement)	4.27	0.65	4.17	0.76	3,186	3.37	0.001
All staff encourage learners to see mistakes as learning opportunities	4.29	0.89	4.21	0.96	3,186	2.63	0.008
All staff support learners to participate in learning activities to their full potential	4.47	0.67	4.41	0.69	3,186	2.49	0.013
All staff encourage learners to be independent and responsible for themselves	4.50	0.81	4.39	0.87	3,186	4.42	<0.001
Procedures for dealing with discriminatory language and attitudes are always followed	4.33	0.59	4.24	0.62	3,186	3.07	0.002
Conflicts/violent incidents are resolved promptly	4.62	0.59	4.60	0.67	3,186	0.98	0.369
Learners can talk to school staff about personal problems that affect their learning	4.49	0.70	4.47	0.74	3,186	3.74	<0.001

M – arithmetic mean; SD – standard deviation; U – Mann-Whitney U-test

Table 15. Impact of the school type (state/non-state) on the rating of recognising learners' subjectivity by the teachers surveyed in 2020

Teachers' rating	State school teachers		Non-state school teachers		df	U-test	p
	M	SD	M	SD			
Overall rating							
Learners' subjectivity	53.52	5.15	54.13	5.02	3,186	-2.00	0.045
Specific ratings							
All staff are responsible for the learners' well-being, seeing it as crucial to the learners' success	4.61	0.76	4.61	0.80	3,186	0.08	0.938
All staff perceive learner diversity as an asset to the school	4.33	0.67	4.44	0.73	3,186	-2.83	0.005
School provides support to reduce any barriers to attendance (e.g., bullying, family situation)	4.56	0.76	4.55	0.78	3,186	0.47	0.637
All staff support and encourage positive peer relationships	4.58	0.67	4.63	0.71	3,186	-1.62	0.106
The school climate enables learners to feel a sense of "belonging"	4.58	0.94	4.62	0.84	3,186	-1.07	0.281
The learners' voice is essential for the school community (daily action and directions for improvement)	4.25	0.84	4.31	0.85	3,186	-1.74	0.081
All staff encourage learners to see mistakes as learning opportunities	4.26	0.75	4.37	0.79	3,186	-2.84	0.005
All staff support learners to participate in learning activities to their full potential	4.46	0.62	4.50	0.70	3,186	-1.41	0.159
All staff encourage learners to be independent and responsible for themselves	4.48	0.68	4.53	0.70	3,186	-1.53	0.127
Procedures for dealing with discriminatory language and attitudes are always followed	4.31	0.67	4.38	0.78	3,186	-2.04	0.041
Conflicts/violent incidents are resolved promptly	4.62	0.67	4.62	0.74	3,186	-2.21	0.919
Learners can talk to school staff about personal problems that affect their learning	4.48	0.98	4.57	0.97	3,186	-2.50	0.012

M – arithmetic mean; SD – standard deviation; U – Mann-Whitney U-test

Characteristically, the level of education taught by the teachers surveyed in 2020 did not statistically significantly differentiate their rating of recognising subjectivity in inclusive education ($M_{\text{pre-school teachers}}$=53.75, SD=5.39; $M_{\text{primary school levels 1 to 3 teachers}}$=54.09, SD=5.21; $M_{\text{primary school levels 4 to 8 teachers}}$=54.19, SD=5.32; $M_{\text{all primary schools levels teachers}}$=53.44, SD=5.07; $M_{\text{secondary school teachers}}$=53.54, SD=5.00; F=1.28; p=0.275).

Learners' subjectivity as rated by the teachers surveyed in 2022 – importance of sociodemographic as well as job- and employment-related variables

The group of teachers surveyed in 2022 differs in terms of recognising the subjectivity of learners in inclusive education, taking into account certain sociodemographic as well as occupation- and employment-related variables. Having said that, these findings indicate a slightly different rating of learners' subjectivity by this group of teachers compared to the ratings expressed by the teachers surveyed in 2020. For example, the teachers' gender turned out to be a non-significant factor for the rating analysed here ($M_{\text{female teachers}}$=51.06, SD=6.30, $M_{\text{male teachers}}$=50.71; Mann-Whitney U=1.17, p=0.317). The teachers' age correlated significantly (albeit weakly) with their rating of learners' subjectivity in inclusive education. Higher ratings were associated with older teachers (r=0.17; p<0.001). In turn, the place of residence did not significantly differentiate the rating of recognising learners' subjectivity in in inclusive education in this group of teachers ($M_{\text{urban teachers}}$=50.88, SD=6.55, $M_{\text{rural teachers}}$=51.26, SD=5.89, t=-1.54, p=0.123). The rating expressed in this respect correlated significantly and positively (albeit weakly) with both seniority and length of service at the current place of employment. Higher ratings with regard to recognising learners' subjectivity in inclusive education were associated with longer seniority (r=0.141, p=0.018) and longer length of service at the current school (r=0.211, p<0.001). The analysis also showed that teachers from state and non-state schools did not differ statistically significantly in their rating of learners' subjectivity in inclusive education ($M_{\text{state school teachers}}$=51.00, SD=6.26, $M_{\text{non-state school teachers}}$=51.19, SD=7.01, Mann-Whitney U=-0.33, p=0.742).

However, in contrast to the group of teachers surveyed in 2020, this group of teachers displayed statistically significant differences in their rating of the recognition of learners' subjectivity in inclusive education depending on the level of education taught. The results of the analysis performed in this area are presented in Table 16. Teachers of all primary school levels rated this subjectivity highest, significantly higher compared to all the other teacher groups. These teachers also scored significantly higher when rating specific aspects of learners' subjectivity in inclusive education. Compared to pre-school, primary school levels 1 to 3, primary school levels 4 to 8 and secondary school teachers, they expressed a significantly higher rating with regard to the following: the school providing support aimed at reducing any barriers (e. g., family-related) experienced by the learner in school attendance; all staff supporting and encouraging positive peer relationships between learners. In terms of the aspect of learner subjectivity expressed as the school climate enabling learners to maintain a sense of "belonging", the lowest scores were obtained by primary school levels 1 to 3 teachers, differing statistically significantly from pre-school teachers, teachers of all primary school levels, and secondary school teachers. Recognising that the learners' voice is decisive for the school community, mainly for taking day-to-day actions, including remedial measures, was particularly appreciated by teachers at primary schools covering all levels, compared to pre-school, primary school levels 1 to 3, and primary school levels 4 to 8 teachers. This group of teachers also rated significantly higher the aspect of prompt resolution of conflicts and violent incidents among learners compared to the other teacher groups. These teachers also scored significantly higher on the aspect of learners' subjectivity consisting in all staff encouraging learners to be independent and responsible for themselves, compared to primary school levels 1 to 3, primary school levels 4 to 8, and secondary school teachers. Compared to pre-school, primary school levels 1 to 3 and primary school levels 4 to 8 teachers, they rated much higher the aspect consisting in learners having the possibility to talk to school staff about personal problems affecting their learning.

Table 16. Impact of the level taught on the rating of recognising learners' subjectivity by the teachers surveyed in 2022

Rating	Pre-school teachers (1)		Teachers of primary school levels 1 to 3 (2)		Teachers of primary school levels 4 to 8 (3)		Teachers of all primary school levels (4)		Secondary school teachers (5)		One-way ANOVA		
	M	SD	M	SD	M	SD	M	SD	M	SD	F	Inter-group comparison	p
Overall rating													
Learners' subjectivity	50.84	7.11	50.51	6.27	50.58	6.28	51.70	6.72	51.00	6.49	3.97*	1–4 2–4 3–4 4–5	0.020 0.001 0.002 0.044
Specific ratings													
1	4.46	0.65	4.37	0.64	4.40	0.60	4.37	0.56	4.40	0.66	3.20*	1–2 2–4 3–4 4–5	0.025 0.002 0.032 0.025
2	4.05	0.87	4.00	0.83	3.00	0.81	4.09	0.79	4.10	0.84	2.10	–	
3	4.31	0.74	4.37	0.65	4.34	0.65	4.46	0.60	4.39	0.64	5.16***	1–4 2–4 3–4 4–5	<0.001 0.013 0.001 0.039
4	4.39	0.68	4.40	0.65	4.36	0.58	4.48	0.63	4.40	0.62	3.55**	1–4 2–4 3–4 4–5	0.022 0.019 0.001 0.030

Table 16 (Continued)

Rating	Pre-school teachers (1) M	SD	Teachers of primary school levels 1 to 3 (2) M	SD	Teachers of primary school levels 4 to 8 (3) M	SD	Teachers of all primary school levels (4) M	SD	Secondary school teachers (5) M	SD	One-way ANOVA F	Inter-group comparison	p
5	4.43	0.70	4.31	0.68	4.37	0.65	4.48	0.72	4.42	0.69	5.96***	1-2 2-4 2-5 3-4 4-5	0.003 <0.001 0.008 0.003 0.008
6	3.93	0.78	3.93	0.73	3.95	0.70	4.03	0.68	4.01	0.64	2.86*	1-4 2-4 2-5 3-4	0.014 0.010 0.049 0.045
7	4.00	0.79	4.01	0.68	3.99	0.69	4.07	0.72	4.09	0.65	1.17	-	
8	4.18	0.69	4.16	0.76	4.21	0.59	4.26	0.73	4.19	0.69	1.83	-	
9	4.27	0.77	4.23	0.67	4.24	0.72	4.32	0.59	4.21	0.65	2.64*	2-4 3-4 4-5	0.020 0.030 0.005
10	4.16	0.64	4.07	0.70	4.03	0.69	4.12	0.55	4.08	0.72	2.33	-	
11	4.38	0.70	4.37	0.67	4.39	0.68	4.52	0.69	4.41	0.73	6.06***	1-4 2-4 3-4 4-5	<0.001 <0.001 <0.001 0.003

Table 16 (Continued)

Rating	Pre-school teachers (1)		Teachers of primary school levels 1 to 3 (2)		Teachers of primary school levels 4 to 8 (3)		Teachers of all primary school levels (4)		Secondary school teachers (5)		One-way ANOVA		
	M	SD	M	SD	M	SD	M	SD	M	SD	F	Inter-group comparison	p
12	4.27	0.69	4.30	0.59	4.33	0.71	4.42	0.65	4.36	0.68	5.11***	1–4 1–5 2–4 3–4	<0.001 0.033 0.001 0.010

1. All staff are responsible for the learners' well-being, seeing it as crucial to the learners' success; 2. All staff perceive learner diversity as an asset to the school; 3. School provides support to reduce any barriers to attendance (e.g., bullying, family situation); 4. All staff support and encourage positive peer relationships; 5. The school climate enables learners to feel a sense of "belonging"; 6. The learners' voice is essential for the school community (daily action and directions for improvement); 7. All staff encourage learners to see mistakes as learning opportunities; 8. All staff support learners to participate in learning activities to their full potential; 9. All staff encourage learners to be independent and responsible for themselves; 10. Procedures for dealing with discriminatory language and attitudes are always followed; 11. Conflicts/violent incidents are resolved promptly; 12. Learners can talk to school staff about personal problems that affect their learning

Conclusion and discussion

Learners' subjectivity is a particularly relevant category in pedagogical theory and educational practice. Consequently, many theoretical dissertations were devoted to it in the past, and numerous concepts were developed linking it for instance to causality and personal autonomy and the relationships between the learner (tutee) and teacher (tutor) (Dubas, 2017). Thus, in these approaches, subjectivity can be treated as a quality (trait, property, attribute) and/or as a process (event/phenomenon – relationship) (Spendel, 1991). The analytical perspective adopted takes into account both approaches indicated, which are combined in pedagogical practice and together form the basis underlying interventions aimed at building and realising learners' subjectivity in school education. They are therefore oriented towards building full participation of all learners in mainstream education. Potential indicators of this participation are the following:
- unrestricted (culturally, mentally, physically) interactions with other participants of the education process;
- unhampered access to valuable social roles within the class team and the school;
- free use of all spaces and tools employed in the education process;
- physical presence in the central space of the classroom (not a required indicator);
- full participation in activities undertaken by all learners (including following instructions and answering questions directed to the whole class) (Gajdzica, 2019).

Making sure that all learners fully participate in mainstream education fits into the broad category of caring for the learners' well-being, and also involves full respect of their rights as individuals (Jarosz, 2013). Looking after the well-being of every learner and their participation in the broad school community is the responsibility of all those working in school, which is why this aspect is reflected in the assertions analysed below.

We analysed recognising learners' subjectivity in inclusive education, similarly as in the case of the beliefs about the validity of this type of education, taking into account the variables adopted, assumed to be relevant for the teachers' ratings. The recognition of learners' subjectivity in inclusive education adopted in the measurement is linked to an indication of the extent to which the well-being of each learner is taken into account in the educational process, as well as to an emphasis on specific levels of functioning of the school and its staff, proving that all learners are respected. The well-being of every learner should unquestionably be respected in inclusive education. It is a core idea, forming the framework for thinking about education covering learners with diverse needs and capabilities who require individualised support. However, the practical implementation of inclusive education may reveal that, in the concrete instances of deployment of such education, continuing to pursue this lofty concept may prove not so much difficult as subject to reflection as to whether the well-being of each child is actually recognised and to what extent, with full acceptance of their subjective treatment throughout the educational process.

The analysis performed showed significantly lower ratings in terms of recognising the subjectivity of each learner in inclusive education among the teachers surveyed in 2022. The significant differences between the groups of teachers surveyed in the two periods (2020 and 2022) suggest the operation of certain factors undermining previous beliefs that inclusive education, the staff involved in it and the school organisation would make it possible (at least to some extent) to practically implement the idea of ensuring the well-being of every learner. It can be assumed that it was not so much the belief that subjective treatment and learners' well-being is important in the educational process that underwent transformation, but rather that increasingly few instruments, means or conditions started to be available within inclusive education that would make it possible to highlight the priority of learners' well-being. Other factors, cited in the previous chapter, were likely to have been at play here too, demonstrating the general work overload of teachers associated with the sudden emergence of many new challenges related to teaching children from war refugee families (Aydin & Kaya, 2019; Soylu, Kaysılı, & Sever, 2020; Pyżalski, 2022).

The sociodemographic and occupation- and employment-related variables taken into account outline a certain, albeit certainly not exhaustive interpretative context for the teachers' rating of the recognition of learners' subjectivity in inclusive education. The teachers' gender differentiated these ratings, but only among the teachers surveyed in 2020. Female teachers, in contrast to male teachers, rated the recognition of learners' subjectivity in inclusive education significantly higher. Indeed, they rated higher almost all specific aspects related to respecting the learners' well-being on different planes of the educational process implemented. It is worth noting the importance of the age variable, which showed different associations among the teachers surveyed in 2020 (negative correlation) and among those surveyed in 2022 (positive correlation). In turn, the place of residence did not differentiate the teachers' ratings of the recognition of learners' subjectivity in inclusive education, regardless of the period in which they were surveyed.

Seniority and length of service at the current place of work correlated positively (albeit weakly) with the teachers' ratings summarised here, but only in the case of those surveyed in 2022. Higher ratings of the recognition of learners' subjectivity in inclusive education were recorded in teachers with longer seniority and longer length of service at their current school. The type of school they were employed at proved to be a factor significantly differentiating their ratings in the area discussed here. However, this was the case only for the group of teachers surveyed in 2020. Teachers employed at non-state schools expressed a significantly higher rating, both in a general sense and in certain specific aspects of recognising learner subjectivity in inclusive education. They emphasised significantly more strongly, for example, that all staff would perceive learner diversity as an asset to the school, and reinforce all learners in the belief that making mistakes is natural and should be used as an opportunity to learn something valuable. They emphasised more strongly that learners had the opportunity to engage in systematic conversations with school staff about personal problems that might affect their learning and outcomes. In contrast, the level of education taught significantly differentiated the teachers' ratings of the recognition of learners' subjectivity only among those surveyed in 2022. The highest scores were recorded for teachers at primary schools covering all levels, who expressed significantly higher ratings compared to all other teacher groups. In contrast to other teachers, they particularly highlighted the aspect of the school providing support oriented towards reducing any barriers to learners' effective learning, as well as the school's practice of encouraging positive relationships with peers. They also emphasised much more strongly the importance of the learners' voice for the corrective actions designed, which is probably related to the teachers of younger learners being more responsible for education in the sense of upbringing, not only teaching (implementation of the curriculum), which is the case of secondary school teachers (Bałachowicz, 2017).

Taking into account the results of the analyses performed, it is concluded that the teachers' rating of the recognition of learners' subjectivity in inclusive education is differentiated in diverse ways by sociodemographic variables and those related to occupation and employment, depending on the period in which the respective teachers were surveyed. The certain ambiguity revealed here in the relationships between the variables revealed makes it possible to conjecture about additional factors, which were not taken into account in this research project, but which may be significant (or even more significant) for the ratings expressed by the teachers concerning the recognition of learners' subjectivity in inclusive education.

Chapter 6.
Support for education/in inclusive education as rated by teachers

Supporting learners' learning as rated by teachers – comparative analysis of 2020 and 2022 study results

An inherent element of inclusive education is support, being an integral part of its structure and, to a significant extent, of its functions, expressed in many levels of learner functioning. Support in inclusive education is seen as multidimensional: it may be seen as related to the learners' learning process as well as to those involved in the learners' education, including teachers. The teachers' rating of the two dimensions of support will be analysed in this chapter, taking into account selected sociodemographic variables (gender, age, place of residence) as well as occupational and employment-related factors (seniority, length of service at the current place of employment, type of school and level of education taught). A key element in the analyses will involve comparing the ratings of support for the learning process of learners and teaching staff given by the teachers surveyed in 2020 and those surveyed in 2022. The analysis showed that the two groups of teachers differed statistically significantly in their rating of the support given to learners by teachers in the learning process. The results obtained in this area are presented in Table 17. The teachers surveyed in 2020 rated support of learners' learning significantly higher than the teachers surveyed in 2022. It is worth emphasising that the differences found are not only highly statistically significant, but also have a large effect size, both in the overall rating and in the specific ratings concerning concrete areas of support provided in the learners' learning process. Taking into account the effect size established, the teachers surveyed in 2020, compared to those surveyed in 2022, were found to rate the support provided by teachers to learners significantly higher in the following aspects: flexibility of collaboration between subject teachers and specialists; teachers working with specialists to meet the individual needs of all learners; recognising learners' needs for support and necessary adaptations; quick and adequate identification of learners' underachievement, taking into account all factors influencing the learners' learning process.

Analysis of the second of the two dimensions of support considered also showed statistically significant differences between the rating expressed by the teachers surveyed in 2020 and those surveyed in 2022 (Table 18). Teachers in the former group scored significantly higher in their ratings of the support of the staff involved in inclusive education. These results relate both to the overall rating and to the specific ratings concerning the multiple different levels of the teaching staff's activity. Just like in the case of the ratings concerning support to the learners' learning, within this dimension of support the differences found were not only highly statistically significant, but also the effect size recorded was medium and large. The teachers surveyed in 2020 rated the support of staff involved in inclusive education significantly higher in the following areas: acting as leaders; participating in activities aimed at improving the learning process and developing achievements in the school community; sharing knowledge and skills with regard to inclusive education; proper training of school management staff as part of school promotion and development focused on the positive outcomes of all learners.

Table 17. Support of learners' learning as rated by the teachers surveyed in 2020 and 2022

Teachers' rating	Teachers surveyed in 2020		Teachers surveyed in 2022		df	t-test	p	Cohen's d
	M	SD	M	SD				
Overall rating								
Support of learners' learning	33.36	3.70	31.84	4.37	6,039	14.60	<0.001	0.857
Specific ratings								
All individuals involved in the education process recognise learners' needs in terms of support and appropriate adaptations	4.29	0.65	4.01	0.78	6,039	15.10	<0.001	1.033
Teachers use a number of assessment methods to confirm their judgments concerning the need to adapt the learning conditions or to include additional resources at the classroom level	4.15	0.61	3.97	0.70	6,039	10.20	<0.001	0.905
Teachers use a number of approaches/strategies to provide additional support, if required, to learners (e.g., universal projects, peer support, tutorship/mentoring)	4.16	0.60	3.99	0.71	6,039	9.45	<0.001	0.786
Teachers use appropriate resources and technologies to improve access to learning	4.32	0.56	4.20	0.67	6,039	8.37	<0.001	0.702
Teachers collaborate and make plans with others (staff/specialists) to meet learners' individual needs	4.38	0.61	4.21	0.72	6,039	10.71	<0.001	1.050
Teachers' roles are flexible (e.g., specialists and subject teachers can alternate in class work)	4.82	0.65	4.53	0.69	6,039	12.25	<0.001	1.342
Teachers are involved in the process of formal assessment of learners' functioning at the school/local level (e.g., identification of special educational needs)	4.32	0.55	4.18	0.61	6,039	8.51	<0.001	0.785
Procedures are in place for identifying cases of learners underachieving, taking into account all factors that affect the learning process – as soon as they emerge.	3.92	0.78	3.73	0.75	6,039	9.41	<0.001	1.022

M – arithmetic mean; SD – standard deviation; t – Student's t-test for independent data

Table 18. Support for teachers involved in inclusive education as rated by the teachers surveyed in 2020 and 2022

Teachers' rating	Teachers surveyed in 2020		Teachers surveyed in 2022		df	t-test	p	Cohen's d
	M	SD	M	SD				
Overall rating								
Support for staff involved in inclusive education	33.51	3.83	31.87	4.71	6,040	14.90	<0.001	0.641
Specific ratings								
Staff are supported in engaging hard-to-reach families to cooperate	3.96	0.77	3.78	0.66	6,040	8.44	<0.001	0.548
School staff are encouraged to participate in activities aimed at improving learning and developing achievements in the school community	3.92	0.77	3.68	0.87	6,040	11.57	<0.001	0.864
Staff have the possibility of sharing knowledge, experience and reflections with their colleagues, the whole process being a form of professional development	4.22	0.63	4.00	0.72	6,040	12.20	<0.001	0.793
Staff act as leaders (e.g., launching new initiatives/innovative curricula)	4.02	0.77	3.67	1.06	6,040	15.12	<0.001	1.026
Staff have access to support for their own needs in challenging situations	4.28	0.62	4.14	0.69	6,040	8.16	<0.001	0.432
Management staff are supported by colleagues at their school	4.49	0.53	4.36	0.45	6,040	9.23	<0.001	0.432
Management staff receive support from external partners/networks (e.g., other schools, universities)	4.42	0.54	4.26	0.66	6,040	10.38	<0.001	0.576
School management staff receive appropriate training with regard to school promotion and development, with a focus on positive outcomes for all learners	4.21	0.54	3.99	0.66	6,040	12.43	<0.001	0.793

M – arithmetic mean; SD – standard deviation; t – Student's t-test for independent data

Support of learners' learning and of staff involved in inclusive education as rated by the teachers surveyed in 2020 – importance of sociodemographic as well as job- and employment-related variables

The analyses performed were studied to check whether the rating of the respective dimensions of support of inclusive education was associated with gender, age and place of residence of the teachers surveyed in 2020. The results indicate that gender is a differentiating factor in the rating of support of learners' learning expressed by this group of teachers (Table 19). Female teachers rated the support provided significantly higher compared to male teachers. They also gave significantly higher ratings to more specific aspects related to the learners' learning process in education for all. In contrast to male teachers, female teachers rated significantly more positively particular aspects of supporting the learners, including: recognising learners' needs for support and necessary facilities; adapting learning conditions or incorporating additional resources at the classroom level; applying additional support elements when necessary; specialists and teachers working together to meet learners' individual needs; participating in the formal assessment of learners' functioning in the school environment.

In terms of the ratings of the support of staff involved in inclusive education, female teachers also scored significantly higher than male teachers. The former also gave significantly higher ratings than the latter in terms of the following specific aspects of support: supporting each other among colleagues with knowledge, reflections and experience; acting as leaders; using support according to one's own needs in challenging situations encountered; receiving support from the school management staff and from external partners, e. g. from other schools.

The age of the teachers surveyed in 2020 did not correlate statistically significantly with either the rating of support of learners' learning (r=-0.121; p=0.712) or the rating of support of staff involved in inclusive education (r=0.042; p=0.813). In turn, statistically significant diversity was found between teachers living in urban and rural areas in both support dimensions analysed. The results obtained in this area are presented in Tables 21 and 22.

Table 19. Impact of teachers' gender on the rating of support of learners' learning by the teachers surveyed in 2020

Teachers' rating	Female teachers		Male teachers		df	U-test	p
	M	SD	M	SD			
Overall rating							
Support of learners' learning	33.34	3.69	32.94	3.92	3,185	2.95	0.003
Specific ratings							
All individuals involved in the education process recognise learners' needs in terms of support and appropriate adaptations	4.31	0.65	4.19	0.66	3,185	3.99	<0.001
Teachers use a number of assessment methods to confirm their judgments concerning the need to adapt the learning conditions or to include additional resources at the classroom level	4.16	0.61	4.08	0.58	3,185	2.77	0.006
Teachers use a number of approaches/strategies to provide additional support, if required, to learners (e.g., universal projects, peer support, tutorship/mentoring)	4.18	0.62	4.07	0.63	3,185	3.82	<0.001
Teachers use appropriate resources and technologies to improve access to learning	4.33	0.58	4.27	0.62	3,185	1.46	0.143
Teachers collaborate and make plans with others (staff/specialists) to meet learners' individual needs	4.40	0.67	4.30	0.69	3,185	3.85	<0.001
Teachers' roles are flexible (e.g., specialists and subject teachers can alternate in class work)	3.81	0.79	3.88	0.82	3,185	-1.86	0.063
Teachers are involved in the process of formal assessment of learners' functioning at the school/local level (e.g., identification of special educational needs)	4.33	0.56	4.26	0.64	3,185	2.62	0.009
Procedures are in place for identifying cases of learners underachieving, taking into account all factors that affect the learning process – as soon as they emerge.	3.93	0.66	3.86	0.71	3,185	1.89	0.058

M – arithmetic mean; SD – standard deviation; U – Mann-Whitney U-test

Table 20. Impact of teachers' gender on the rating of support for staff involved in inclusive education by the teachers surveyed in 2020

Teachers' rating	Female teachers		Male teachers		df	U-test	p
	M	SD	M	SD			
Overall rating							
Support for staff involved in inclusive education	33.58	3.85	33.17	3.72	3,186	4.12	0.017
Specific ratings							
Staff are supported in engaging hard-to-reach families to cooperate	3.95	0.78	3.99	0.72	3,186	-0.94	0.345
School staff are encouraged to participate in activities aimed at improving learning and developing achievements in the school community	3.92	0.69	3.93	0.71	3,186	-0.33	0.714
Staff have the possibility of sharing knowledge, experience and reflections with their colleagues, the whole process being a form of professional development	4.23	0.65	4.17	0.67	3,186	2.00	0.045
Staff act as leaders (e.g., launching new initiatives/innovative curricula)	4.03	0.76	3.95	0.79	3,186	2.34	0.019
Staff have access to support for their own needs in challenging situations	4.30	0.67	4.17	0.64	3,186	4.47	<0.001
Management staff are supported by colleagues at their school	4.51	0.56	4.42	0.59	3,186	3.35	0.001
Management staff receive support from external partners/networks (e.g., other schools, universities)	4.43	0.65	4.37	0.67	3,186	2.44	0.015
School management staff receive appropriate training with regard to school promotion and development, with a focus on positive outcomes for all learners	4.22	0.68	4.17	0.72	3,186	1.91	0.056

M – arithmetic mean; SD – standard deviation; U –Mann-Whitney U-test

Table 21. Impact of teachers' place of residence on the rating of support of learners' learning by the teachers surveyed in 2020

Teachers' rating	Urban teachers		Rural teachers		df	t-test	p	Cohen's d
	M	SD	M	SD				
Overall rating								
Support of learners' learning	33.52	3.78	33.07	3.52	3,185	3.26	0.001	0.545
Specific ratings								
All individuals involved in the education process recognise learners' needs in terms of support and appropriate adaptations	4.32	0.67	4.25	0.66	3,185	2.76	0.006	0.599
Teachers use a number of assessment methods to confirm their judgments concerning the need to adapt the learning conditions or to include additional resources at the classroom level	4.17	0.89	4.11	0.92	3,185	2.41	0.016	0.685
Teachers use a number of approaches/strategies to provide additional support, if required, to learners (e.g., universal projects, peer support, tutorship/mentoring)	4.19	0.72	4.11	0.67	3,185	3.24	0.001	0.514
Teachers use appropriate resources and technologies to improve access to learning	4.34	0.67	4.29	0.69	3,185	2.38	0.017	0.428
Teachers collaborate and make plans with others (staff/specialists) to meet learners' individual needs	4.41	0.71	4.34	0.77	3,185	3.42	0.001	0.598
Teachers' roles are flexible (e.g., specialists and subject teachers can alternate in class work)	3.82	0.67	3.82	0.70	3,185	0.25	0.802	-
Teachers are involved in the process of formal assessment of learners' functioning at the school/local level (e.g., identification of special educational needs)	4.32	0.87	4.30	0.86	3,185	1.16	0.245	-
Procedures are in place for identifying cases of learners underachieving, taking into account all factors that affect the learning process – as soon as they emerge.	3.95	0.65	3.86	0.64	3,185	3.56	<0.001	0.771

M – arithmetic mean; SD – standard deviation; t – Student's t-test for independent data

Table 22. Impact of teachers' place of residence on the rating of support for staff involved in inclusive education by the teachers surveyed in 2020

Teachers' rating	Urban teachers		Rural teachers		df	t-test	p	Cohen's d
	M	SD	M	SD				
Overall rating								
Support for staff involved in inclusive education	33.67	3.90	33.25	3.71	3,186	2.98	0.003	0.259
Specific ratings								
Staff are supported in engaging hard-to-reach families to cooperate	4.23	0.57	4.18	0.67	3,186	2.50	0.012	0.291
School staff are encouraged to participate in activities aimed at improving learning and developing achievements in the school community	4.44	0.87	4.38	0.92	3,186	3.13	0.002	0.362
Staff have the possibility of sharing knowledge, experience and reflections with their colleagues, the whole process being a form of professional development	4.52	0.69	4.45	0.72	3,186	3.51	<0.001	0.413
Staff act as leaders (e.g., launching new initiatives/innovative curricula)	4.31	0.76	4.23	0.78	3,186	3.29	0.001	0.472
Staff have access to support for their own needs in challenging situations	4.05	0.59	3.96	0.62	3,186	2.93	0.003	0.531
Management staff are supported by colleagues at their school	4.22	0.66	4.21	0.68	3,186	0.20	0.845	-
Management staff receive support from external partners/networks (e.g., other schools, universities)	3.93	0.89	3.91	0.92	3,186	0.85	0.397	-
School management staff receive appropriate training with regard to school promotion and development, with a focus on positive outcomes for all learners	3.97	0.90	3.93	0.88	3,186	1.51	0.130	-

M – arithmetic mean; SD – standard deviation; t – Student's t-test for independent data

The analysis showed that teachers from urban areas rated the support of learners' learning significantly higher than teachers from rural areas, with a medium effect size. They rated learning support significantly higher with regard to several specific aspects, except only two related to supporting flexibility of the roles fulfilled by teachers and specialists in the classroom and teachers' participation in the formal assessment of learners' functioning in the school environment. The effect of the differences found here is at a medium level. Urban teachers also rated the support provided to staff involved in the implementation of inclusive education significantly higher. A weak effect size was recorded for this difference. Urban teachers gave significantly higher specific ratings concerning the various levels of support. With a weak and medium effect size of the difference, teachers in this group rated support significantly higher in the following areas: supporting staff to start working with learners' families; participating in activities oriented towards the learning processes; sharing knowledge and experience with each other; acting as leaders; and meeting individual needs in challenging situations encountered.

An analysis of the significance of occupation- and employment-related variables revealed that seniority and length of service at the current school did not correlate significantly with either the rating of support of learners' learning ($r=0.032$, $p=0.070$; $r=0.001$, $p=0.938$, respectively) or the rating of support of staff involved in inclusive education as expressed by the teachers surveyed in 2020 ($r=0.003$, $p=0.962$; $r=0.002$, $p=0.932$, respectively). In turn, the type of school in which the teacher taught differentiated statistically significantly the group of teachers surveyed in 2020 in their rating of support of learners' learning (Table 23). No statistically significant difference was found, however, in the rating of support of staff involved in inclusive education: $M_{state\ school\ teachers}=33.51$, $SD=3.81$; $M_{non\text{-}state\ school\ teachers}=33.52$, $SD=3.97$; Mann-Whitney $U=-0.14$, $p=0.966$. In the case of rating of support of learners' learning, teachers from non-state schools scored significantly higher compared to teachers from state schools. Teachers from non-state schools gave significantly higher ratings with regard to the following aspects of support: adapting learning conditions or additional resources at the classroom level; providing additional support according to learners' individual needs; using appropriate resources and technologies to enhance learning opportunities; specialists and subject teachers working together to meet the diverse needs of all learners; flexibility of the roles fulfilled by subject teachers and specialists.

Table 23. Impact of the school type (state/non-state) on the rating of support of learners' learning by the teachers surveyed in 2020

Teachers' rating	State school teachers		Non-state school teachers		df	U-test	p
	M	SD	M	SD			
Overall rating							
Support of learners' learning	33.30	3.60	33.86	3.71	3,185	-2.58	0.010
Specific ratings							
All individuals involved in the education process recognise learners' needs in terms of support and appropriate adaptations	4.29	0.66	4.33	0.59	3,185	-1.18	0.238
Teachers use a number of assessment methods to confirm their judgments concerning the need to adapt the learning conditions or to include additional resources at the classroom level	4.14	0.61	4.23	0.60	3,185	-2.15	0.012
Teachers use a number of approaches/strategies to provide additional support, if required, to learners (e.g., universal projects, peer support, tutorship/mentoring)	4.15	0.63	4.26	0.60	3,185	-3.17	0.002
Teachers use appropriate resources and technologies to improve access to learning	4.32	0.55	4.40	0.54	3,185	-2.49	0.013
Teachers collaborate and make plans with others (staff/specialists) to meet learners' individual needs	4.37	0.86	4.45	0.87	3,185	-2.20	0.028
Teachers' roles are flexible (e.g., specialists and subject teachers can alternate in class work)	3.81	0.65	3.95	0.69	3,185	-2.93	0.003
Teachers are involved in the process of formal assessment of learners' functioning at the school/ local level (e.g., identification of special educational needs)	4.32	0.71	4.27	0.80	3,185	1.56	0.119
Procedures are in place for identifying cases of learners underachieving, taking into account all factors that affect the learning process – as soon as they emerge.	3.91	0.57	3.97	0.66	3,185	-1.26	0.207

M – arithmetic mean; SD – standard deviation; U –Mann-Whitney U-test

The significance of the level of education taught for the rating of the support of learners' learning and for the rating of the staff involved in inclusive education was also analysed. The results obtained in this area are presented in Tables 24 and 25. The variable analysed here differentiates statistically significantly the teachers' rating with regard to the support of learners' learning (Table 24). Pre-school teachers scored significantly higher in the rating expressed here compared to primary school levels 1 to 3 teachers, teachers at primary schools covering all levels, and secondary school teachers. Similar results were obtained by this group of teachers in the rating of four specific levels of support of the learners' learning process: recognising learners' needs with regard to support and the necessary adaptations; adapting the learning conditions and incorporating additional resources at the classroom level; using diverse strategies aimed at providing additional support when necessary; as well as collaboration and joint planning in the team of specialists and subject teachers to meet the individual needs of all learners pursuing compulsory schooling in inclusive education. Pre-school teachers rated these support aspects significantly higher compared to teachers at primary schools covering all levels and secondary school teachers. This group of teachers also gave a significantly higher rating, compared to primary school teachers (of all levels) and secondary school teachers, with regard to the support concerning the flexibility of classroom roles among specialists and subject teachers, and the participation of teachers in the formal assessment of learners' functioning in the school environment.

A different situation was seen in terms of the rating of the other dimension of support, namely that of staff involved in inclusive education. In the overall rating, the teachers surveyed in 2020, differing in terms of the level of education taught, showed similar results (Table 25). A statistically significant difference was only recorded in the rating of the specific aspect of support concerning the support received by management staff from external partners. Secondary schools teachers scored highest here, differing significantly from pre-school teachers, primary school levels 1 to 3 teachers, and teachers at primary schools covering all levels of education.

Table 24. Impact of the level taught on the rating of support of learners' learning by the teachers surveyed in 2020

Rating	Pre-school teachers (1)		Teachers of primary school levels 1 to 3 (2)		Teachers of primary school levels 4 to 8 (3)		Teachers of all primary school levels (4)		Secondary school teachers (5)		One-way ANOVA		
	M	SD	M	SD	M	SD	M	SD	M	SD	F	Inter-group comparison	p
Support of learners' learning													
							Overall rating						
	34.05	3.68	33.39	3.74	34.22	3.99	33.06	3.63	33.09	3.73	11.06***	1-2 / 1-4 / 1-5	0.024 / <0.001 / <0.001
							Specific ratings						
1	4.40	0.63	4.26	0.66	4.33	0.52	4.24	0.66	4.26	0.65	9.18***	1-2 / 1-4 / 1-5	0.007 / <0.001 / <0.001
2	4.25	0.59	4.14	0.61	4.18	0.74	4.10	0.61	4.12	0.67	8.83***	1-2 / 1-4 / 1-5	0.025 / <0.001 / <0.001
3	4.29	0.58	4.17	0.59	4.28	0.65	4.09	0.63	4.12	0.68	14.87***	1-2 / 1-4 / 1-5	0.005 / <0.001 / <0.001
4	4.34	0.57	4.33	0.60	4.38	0.72	4.31	0.66	4.34	0.69	0.60	–	
5	4.48	0.55	4.38	0.59	4.63	0.65	4.35	0.64	4.33	0.67	8.52***	1-2 / 1-4 / 1-5	0.033 / <0.001 / <0.001
6	3.92	0.85	3.83	0.78	3.63	0.81	3.79	0.77	3.75	0.80	4.49**	1-4 / 1-5	<0.001 / <0.001

Table 24 (Continued)

Rating	Pre-school teachers (1)		Teachers of primary school levels 1 to 3 (2)		Teachers of primary school levels 4 to 8 (3)		Teachers of all primary school levels (4)		Secondary school teachers (5)		One-way ANOVA		
	M	SD	M	SD	M	SD	M	SD	M	SD	F	Inter-group comparison	p
7	4.35	0.55	4.32	0.53	4.50	0.60	4.32	0.59	4.27	0.60	2.08	-	
8	4.13	0.69	3.95	0.71	4.02	0.68	3.85	0.69	3.91	0.70	7.39***	1-4 1-5	<0.001 0.004

1: All individuals involved in the education process recognise learners' needs in terms of support and appropriate adaptations; 2: Teachers use a number of assessment methods to confirm their judgments concerning the need to adapt the learning conditions or to include additional resources at the classroom level; 3. Teachers use a number of approaches/strategies to provide additional support, if required, to learners (e.g., universal projects, peer support, tutorship/mentoring); 4: Teachers use appropriate resources and technologies to improve access to learning; 5: Teachers collaborate and make plans with others (staff/specialists) to meet learners' individual needs; 6: Teachers' roles are flexible (e.g., specialists and subject teachers can alternate in class work); 7: Teachers are involved in the process of formal assessment of learners' functioning at the school/local level (e.g., identification of special educational needs); 8: Procedures are in place for identifying cases of learners underachieving, taking into account all factors that affect the learning process – as soon as they emerge.

Table 25. Impact of the level taught on the rating of support for staff involved in inclusive education by the teachers surveyed in 2020

Rating	Pre-school teachers (1)		Teachers of primary school levels 1 to 3 (2)		Teachers of primary school levels 4 to 8 (3)		Teachers of all primary school levels (4)		Secondary school teachers (5)		One-way ANOVA		
	M	SD	M	SD	M	SD	M	SD	M	SD	F	Inter-group comparison	p
Overall rating													
Support for staff involved in inclusive education	33.59	3.95	33.30	3.64	33.87	4.32	33.48	3.71	33.53	3.83	0.27	-	
Specific ratings													
1	4.21	0.64	4.25	0.59	4.38	0.74	4.24	0.60	4.14	0.73	2.85*	-	
2	4.43	0.55	4.42	0.53	4.50	0.60	4.43	0.59	4.39	0.54	0.65	-	
3	4.50	0.52	4.50	0.51	4.50	0.53	4.49	0.54	4.45	0.52	1.24	-	
4	4.31	0.52	4.25	0.51	4.25	0.54	4.27	0.52	4.27	0.55	0.63	-	
5	4.05	0.66	3.98	0.63	4.25	0.61	4.00	0.66	4.02	0.67	0.92	-	
6	4.20	0.65	4.21	0.66	4.25	0.67	4.23	0.64	4.20	0.66	0.40	-	
7	3.92	0.71	3.81	0.80	3.75	0.74	3.89	0.75	4.03	0.76	5.31***	1-5 2-5 4-5	0.005 <0.001 <0.001

Table 25 (Continued)

Rating	Pre-school teachers (1)		Teachers of primary school levels 1 to 3 (2)		Teachers of primary school levels 4 to 8 (3)		Teachers of all primary school levels (4)		Secondary school teachers (5)		One-way ANOVA		
	M	SD	M	SD	M	SD	M	SD	M	SD	F	Inter-group comparison	p
3	3.97	0.78	3.88	0.76	4.00	0.80	3.93	0.77	4.00	0.76	2.30		

1: Staff are supported in engaging hard-to-reach families to cooperate; 2: School staff are encouraged to participate in activities aimed at improving learning and developing achievements in the school community; 3: Staff have the possibility of sharing knowledge, experience and reflections with their colleagues, the whole process being a form of professional development; 4: Staff act as leaders (e.g., launching new initiatives/innovative curricula); 5. Staff have access to support for their own needs in challenging situations; 6: Management staff are supported by colleagues at their school; 7: Management staff receive support from external partners/networks (e.g., other schools, universities) School management staff receive appropriate training with regard to school promotion and development, with a focus on positive outcomes for all learners

Support of learners' learning and of staff involved in inclusive education as rated by the teachers surveyed in 2022 – importance of sociodemographic as well as job- and employment-related variables

The following section contains an analysis, taking into account sociodemographic as well as occupation- and employment-related variables, of the rating of the support of learners' learning and of the support of staff involved in inclusive education expressed by the teachers surveyed in 2022. The results obtained indicate that the teachers' gender is not a differentiating factor in their rating either of the support of learners' learning in education for all ($M_{female\ teachers}$=31.86, SD=4.37, $M_{male\ teachers}$=31.68, SD=4.44, Mann-Whitney U=0.79, p=0.718), or of the support of staff involved in inclusive education ($M_{female\ teachers}$=31.84, SD=4.72, $M_{male\ teachers}$=32.07, SD=4.60, Mann-Whitney U=-0.89, p=0.373). The age of the teachers in this group is not statistically significantly associated with their rating of the support of the learners' learning process (r=-0.035, p=0.134). In turn, significant (albeit weak) correlations were found between the age of the teachers and their rating of the support of staff involved in inclusive education. Higher ratings of this dimension of education for all were associated with older teachers (r=0.191; p=0.001). The third sociodemographic variable considered, i. e. place of residence, appeared to significantly differentiate the teachers' rating of support, but only in the dimension of support of staff involved in inclusive education. The results indicate that teachers from rural areas rate this type of support significantly higher compared to teachers from urban areas, with the effect size found to be relatively weak (Table 26). Teachers from rural areas rated support significantly higher in three specific aspects: support in engaging learners' families to cooperate; support of the school management staff by collaborators/ colleagues; and appropriate training with regard to school promotion and development, with a focus on the achievement of positive outcomes by all learners. In terms of the rating of support of learners' learning, the teachers' place of residence was found to be statistically insignificant ($M_{urban\ teachers}$=31.83, SD=4.52; $M_{rural\ teachers}$=31.84, SD=4.12, t=-1.12, p=0.264).

Table 26. Impact of teachers' place of residence on the rating of support for staff involved in inclusive education by the teachers surveyed in 2022

Teachers' rating	Urban teachers		Rural teachers		df	t-test	p	Cohen's d
	M	SD	M	SD				
Overall rating								
Support for staff involved in inclusive education	31.74	4.88	32.11	4.40	2,851	-2.02	0.043	0.202
Specific ratings								
Staff are supported in engaging hard-to-reach families to cooperate	3.96	0.80	4.03	0.69	2,851	-2.29	0.022	0.208
School staff are encouraged to participate in activities aimed at improving learning and developing achievements in the school community	4.25	0.68	4.27	0.63	2,851	-0.75	0.456	-
Staff have the possibility of sharing knowledge, experience and reflections with their colleagues, the whole process being a form of professional development	4.34	0.63	4.37	0.58	2,851	-1.18	0.237	-
Staff act as leaders (e.g., launching new initiatives/innovative curricula)	4.15	0.71	4.13	0.64	2,851	0.64	0.522	-
Staff have access to support for their own needs in challenging situations	3.64	0.96	3.71	0.72	2,851	-1.81	0.070	-
Management staff are supported by colleagues at their school	3.97	0.72	4.06	0.70	2,851	-3.07	0.002	0.268
Management staff receive support from external partners/networks (e.g., other schools, universities)	3.66	0.87	3.71	0.86	2,851	-1.32	0.185	-
School management staff receive appropriate training with regard to school promotion and development, with a focus on positive outcomes for all learners	3.75	0.88	3.82	0.82	2,851	-2.10	0.036	0.209

M – arithmetic mean; SD – standard deviation; t – Student's t-test for independent data

The rating of the two dimensions of support of inclusive education by the teachers surveyed in 2022 was also analysed, taking into account variables related to their occupation and employment. The seniority of the teachers in this group is not statistically significantly associated with their rating of the support of the learners' learning process ($r=0.028$, $p=0.139$). In turn, length of service at the current school correlated positively (albeit weakly) with ratings of this dimension of support. Higher ratings given by teachers were associated with their longer length of service at their current place of employment ($r=0.160$, $p<0.001$). In turn, significant and positive (albeit weak) correlations were found in the case of ratings of the support of staff involved in inclusive education, both with seniority ($r=0.210$, $p<0.001$) and with length of service at the current place of employment ($r=0.189$, $p<0.001$). Higher ratings of this dimension of support in inclusive education were associated with longer seniority in general and with longer length of service at the current school. The type of school the teachers were employed at did not significantly differentiate their ratings of the support of the learners' learning process ($M_{\text{state school teachers}}=31.83$; $SD=4.33$; $M_{\text{non-state school teachers}}=31.92$; $SD=5.18$; Mann-Whitney $U=-0.24$; $p=0.810$). No significant difference was recorded either in the case of the rating of the support of staff involved in inclusive education ($M_{\text{state school teachers}}=31.87$; $SD=4.67$; $M_{\text{non-state school teachers}}=31.85$; $SD=5.46$; Mann-Whitney $U=0.51$; $p=0.959$).

What the analysis results do indicate is that the level of education taught in the case of the teachers surveyed in 2022 was a factor significantly differentiating their rating of the learners' learning process in inclusive education (Table 27). Pre-school teachers scored highest on this rating, significantly higher than primary school levels 1 to 3, primary school levels 4 to 8, and secondary school teachers. Secondary school teachers also rated this type of support significantly lower than teachers of all primary school levels. Significant difference between the teacher groups taken into account was found in the specific ratings of individual aspects of support of learners' learning. It is worth pointing out that pre-school teachers expressed the highest ratings, differing statistically significantly in this respect from the other teacher groups. However, secondary school teachers rated support in the form of teacher participation in formal assessment of learners' functioning in the school environment significantly lowest. In terms of the rating of three aspects of support of learners' learning, no statistically significant differences were found between groups of teachers teaching at different levels: providing learners with additional support; using appropriate resources and technologies aimed at improving access to learning; and identifying learners' underachievement, taking into account all factors influencing the learning process early on as they emerge.

Table 27. Impact of the level taught on the rating of support of learners' learning by the teachers surveyed in 2022

Rating	Pre-school teachers (1)		Teachers of primary school levels 1 to 3 (2)		Teachers of primary school levels 4 to 8 (3)		Teachers of all primary school levels (4)		Secondary school teachers (5)		One-way ANOVA		
	M	SD	M	SD	M	SD	M	SD	M	SD	F	Inter-group comparison	p
Overall rating													
Support of learners' learning	32.41	4.51	31.70	4.29	31.73	4.23	32.06	4.24	31.25	4.60	5.18***	1-2 / 1-3 / 1-5 / 4-5	0.011 / 0.015 / <0.001 / 0.001
Specific ratings													
1	4.11	0.75	3.99	0.77	3.96	0.76	4.07	0.77	3.91	0.86	5.93***	1-2 / 1-3 / 1-5 / 3-4 / 4-5	0.020 / 0.003 / <0.001 / 0.015 / <0.001
2	4.08	0.71	3.96	0.69	3.99	0.66	3.98	0.68	3.88	0.76	4.88***	1-2 / 1-3 / 1-4 / 1-5	0.008 / 0.049 / 0.024 / 0.001
3	4.07	0.73	3.99	0.74	3.99	0.68	4.00	0.69	3.94	0.76	2.09	–	
4	4.18	0.60	4.21	0.61	4.18	0.63	4.21	0.59	4.20	0.60	0.20	–	

Table 27 (Continued)

Rating	Pre-school teachers (1)		Teachers of primary school levels 1 to 3 (2)		Teachers of primary school levels 4 to 8 (3)		Teachers of all primary school levels (4)		Secondary school teachers (5)		One-way ANOVA		
	M	SD	M	SD	M	SD	M	SD	M	SD	F	Inter-group comparison	p
5	4.31	0.66	4.20	0.65	4.19	0.67	4.23	0.68	4.14	0.69	4.25**	1–2 1–3 1–4 1–5 4–5	0.015 0.007 0.043 <0.001 0.014
6	3.61	1.02	3.45	0.95	3.53	0.93	3.60	0.95	3.44	1.03	3.89**	1–2 1–5 2–4 4–5	0.009 0.007 0.005 0.004
7	4.25	0.64	4.19	0.59	4.18	0.60	4.24	0.59	4.08	0.67	6.43***	1–5 2–5 3–5 4–5	<0.001 0.007 0.015 <0.001
8	3.80	0.84	3.72	0.82	3.71	0.81	3.74	0.83	3.66	0.84	2.07	-	

1: All individuals involved in the education process recognise learners' needs in terms of support and appropriate adaptations; 2: Teachers use a number of assessment methods to confirm their judgments concerning the need to adapt the learning conditions or to include additional resources at the classroom level; 3. Teachers use a number of approaches/strategies to provide additional support, if required, to learners (e.g., universal projects, peer support, tutorship/mentoring); 4: Teachers use appropriate resources and technologies to improve access to learning; 5: Teachers collaborate and make plans with others (staff/specialists) to meet learners' individual needs; 6: Teachers' roles are flexible (e.g., specialists and subject teachers can alternate in class work);7: Teachers are involved in the process of formal assessment of learners' functioning at the school/local level (e.g., identification of special educational needs); 8: Procedures are in place for identifying cases of learners underachieving, taking into account all factors that affect the learning process – as soon as they emerge.

Table 28. Impact of the level taught on the rating of support for staff involved in inclusive education by the teachers surveyed in 2022

Rating	Pre-school teachers (1)		Teachers of primary school levels 1 to 3 (2)		Teachers of primary school levels 4 to 8 (3)		Teachers of all primary school levels (4)		Secondary school teachers (5)		One-way ANOVA		
	M	SD	M	SD	M	SD	M	SD	M	SD	F	Inter-group comparison	p
Overall rating													
Support for staff involved in inclusive education	31.75	5.14	31.39	4.58	31.46	4.92	32.53	4.27	31.82	4.80	6.57***	1–4 2–4 3–4 4–5	0.004 <0.001 <0.001 0.006
Specific ratings													
1	3.94	0.79	3.93	0.74	3.97	0.77	4.10	0.71	3.92	0.82	6.37***	1–4 2–4 3–4 4–5	0.001 <0.001 0.004 <0.001
2	4.22	0.70	4.20	0.65	4.22	0.70	4.37	0.61	4.22	0.67	8.08***	1–4 2–4 3–4 4–5	<0.001 <0.001 <0.001 <0.001
3	4.35	0.62	4.30	0.63	4.31	0.64	4.46	0.54	4.30	0.66	9.01***	1–4 2–4 3–4 4–5	0.001 <0.001 <0.001 <0.001

Table 28 (*Continued*)

Rating	Pre-school teachers (1)		Teachers of primary school levels 1 to 3 (2)		Teachers of primary school levels 4 to 8 (3)		Teachers of all primary school levels (4)		Secondary school teachers (5)		One-way ANOVA		
	M	SD	M	SD	M	SD	M	SD	M	SD	F	Inter-group comparison	p
4	4.15	0.72	4.09	0.68	4.12	0.67	4.20	0.66	4.11	0.73	2.88*	2–4 3–4 4–5	0.004 0.024 0.010
5	3.69	1.02	3.56	1.05	3.54	1.06	3.80	0.93	3.69	0.98	7.63***	1–2 1–3 2–4 2–5 3–4 3–5 4–5	0.031 0.015 <0.001 0.035 <0.001 0.016 0.036
6	3.96	0.79	3.95	0.69	3.98	0.75	4.08	0.65	4.00	0.72	3.51**	1–4 2–4 3–4	0.004 0.002 0.013
7	3.68	0.93	3.59	0.84	3.58	0.89	3.71	0.86	3.80	0.82	5.96***	1–5 2–4 2–5 3–4 3–5 4–5	0.024 0.016 <0.001 0.010 <0.001 0.045

Table 28 (Continued)

Rating	Pre-school teachers (1)		Teachers of primary school levels 1 to 3 (2)		Teachers of primary school levels 4 to 8 (3)		Teachers of all primary school levels (4)		Secondary school teachers (5)		One-way ANOVA		
	M	SD	M	SD	M	SD	M	SD	M	SD	F	Inter-group comparison	p
8	3.77	0.89	3.76	0.76	3.75	0.80	3.82	0.81	3.79	0.79	0.70	-	

1: Staff are supported in engaging hard-to-reach families to cooperate; 2: School staff are encouraged to participate in activities aimed at improving learning and developing achievements in the school community; 3: Staff have the possibility of sharing knowledge, experience and reflections with their colleagues, the whole process being a form of professional development; 4: Staff act as leaders (e. g., launching new initiatives/innovative curricula); 5. Staff have access to support for their own needs in challenging situations; 6: Management staff are supported by colleagues at their school; 7: Management staff receive support from external partners/networks (e. g., other schools, universities) School management staff receive appropriate training with regard to school promotion and development, with a focus on positive outcomes for all learners

Similarly as in the case of rating of the support of learners' learning, teachers teaching at different levels obtained diverse results in terms of the rating of the support of staff involved in inclusive education. Teachers working at primary schools covering all levels of education rated this type of support in inclusive education highest, significantly higher than teachers from all the other teacher groups. In addition, significant differences are found here between the groups of teachers in relation to almost all the specific aspects of support of staff involved in inclusive education, except the dimension that concerns providing appropriate training with regard to school promotion and development, with a focus on the achievement of positive outcomes by all learners. Primary school teachers working at all levels scored highest on this rating, differing statistically significantly from the other teacher groups. Only in the area of support of management staff received from external partners did secondary school teachers score highest, with significantly higher ratings compared to teachers in the other groups.

Conclusion and discussion

Summarising the results obtained in the analyses of teachers' ratings of the support of the learners' learning process and of the support of the staff involved in inclusive education, it is possible to indicate several significant elements showing the complex context of perceiving support, considered as an aspect of inclusive education. In line with the premise, we analysed two dimensions of support, equally important in the organisation and implementation of inclusive education: supporting each learner's learning and supporting the staff involved in this educational process. Similarly as in the case of the previous elements (validity of education for all learners and recognising learners' subjectivity in inclusive education), both dimensions of support taken into account were rated by the teachers surveyed in two periods (2020 and 2022), and in the context of sociodemographic as well as occupation- and employment-related variables. To generally summarise the results obtained, it is worth emphasising that the ratings of the support of the learning process and of the support of the staff involved in inclusive education were differentiated by slightly different factors. This, therefore, not only confirms the different nature of the two dimensions of support, but also suggests we should seek different sources of their explanation and provision. The perception of support by teachers manifested in their ratings is certainly based on their beliefs concerning the kind of support that should be provided for each learner's learning process, or to the staff involved in teaching them. These beliefs, in turn, are shaped by a number of contextual factors embedded in the teacher's personal profile, experiences, place and conditions of work, etc. The set of factors taken into account in the analyses provides important explanatory elements, but the latter are definitely not exhaustive for a full understanding of support in inclusive education. This reveals a certain perspective of teachers outlined by selected sociodemographic and professional traits.

Teachers rated the support for each learner's learning process differently in 2020 and in 2022. Of note is the significantly lower rating of this element of inclusive education among the teachers surveyed in 2022. The large effect size found suggests an actual difference, signalling profound transformations in the possibilities of supporting the learning process of learners with diverse needs as perceived by teachers. The teachers surveyed in 2022 rated significantly lower the areas of support based on the flexibility of collaboration between specialists and subject teachers, effective identification of the needs of all learners, and under-achievement. When attempting to explain these data, it is worth pointing out that the support provided to teachers between 2020 and 2022 was not systemically restricted by any legislation. On the contrary, it was actually intensified due to the emergence of large numbers of learners from refugee families in the education system. Numerous generally available courses/seminars as well as methodo-logical materials aimed at developing competencies to work in a culturally di-verse group appeared, as described in more detail in earlier analyses. The burden, however, changed, and the number of situations perceived by teachers as chal-lenging increased, as illustrated by data from the report cited earlier: *Razem w klasie. Dzieci z Ukrainy w polskich szkołach* (Pyżalski et al., 2022). It can therefore be concluded that, in the perception of the teachers surveyed in 2022, the support they received became more clearly insufficient compared to the support received in the opinion of the teachers surveyed in the first group in 2020. Faced with the significant increase in interculturalism in Polish schools in 2022, there may have been a lack of a well thought-out strategy of building support, from system-wide macrostructures to microstructures in each school and classroom. Research shows that the implementation of fundamental practices such as setting a vision and a direction for change, creating a climate conducive to diversified teaching and learning, building of potential and instructional leadership is of key im-portance in the building of the whole system of support (Okilwa, Jo Cordova, & Haupert, 2022). It is worth mentioning at this point that teachers' perceptions of support correlates positively with a more positive attitude towards educational inclusion (Desombre, Delaval, & Jury, 2021; Werner, S., Gumpel, Koller, Wie-senthal, & Weintraub, 2021), which partly explains the results concerning teachers' opinions on the validity of inclusive education discussed in one of the previous sections.

An analysis of the results showed that the rating of support of learners' learning is subject to differentiation by gender, but only in the group of teachers surveyed in 2020. Indeed, female teachers rated the support of this process more positively, emphasising the importance of identifying the needs of each learner in terms of support, adapting conditions and resources to the needs of individual learners, and teachers working with specialists to meet learners' individual needs. The teachers' age appeared to be insignificant for their rating of the support of the learning process, as opposed to another sociodemographic variable, i. e. the place of residence. Urban teachers rated this dimension of support in inclusive education significantly higher compared to rural teachers.

On the basis of the analysis, we conclude that the rating of the learners' learning support is unrelated to overall seniority. It does, however, shows positive links with length of service at the current place of work of teachers, but only among those surveyed in 2022. The rating of the support of the learners' learning process varied depending on the school the teachers taught at. This is because teachers from non-state schools rated this dimension of support and its individual areas significantly higher, including the areas related to the provision of additional support when required by the learner, adapting the conditions and resources to meet the individual needs of all learners, and using appropriate technological means and possibilities to enhance the learning perspectives. Importantly, the differences indicated were recorded only among the teachers surveyed in 2020. As a result of the analyses, we furthermore conclude that the rating of support of the learners' learning process varies depending on the level taught by the respondents. Significant differences in this respect were found regardless of the period in which the teachers were surveyed. This support was rated highest by pre-school teachers, significantly higher compared to all the other teacher groups.

Support of staff involved in inclusive education was rated differently by the teachers depending on several factors taken into account in the analyses. Similarly as in the case of the rating of the support of each learner's learning process, the teachers surveyed in 2022 also rated this dimension significantly lower. The large effect size found in this area is worth highlighting. The difference recorded between the teachers surveyed in 2020 and in 2022 is significant enough to reflect the profound changes in their perception of the organisation and implementation of inclusive education in Polish schools. Teachers in 2022 were significantly less convinced that staff should act as leaders and be engaged in improving the learning process of all learners. They also rated lower the readiness of staff involved in inclusive education to share knowledge, skills and experience with each other. Teachers in this group appear to maintain much more detachment from potential support activities. The results obtained here may also suggest the clearly weakening mechanisms of the support provided in the implementation of inclusive education, most probably reflecting the inadequacy of that support as the need for it grows, given the increasingly demanding conditions for the education of all learners.

Rating of the support of staff involved in inclusive education appears to be differentiated by gender, but only among the teachers surveyed in 2020. Female teachers rated this type of support significantly higher compared to male teachers, emphasising above all the friendly team spirit when it came to the sharing of knowledge and experience concerning inclusive education among colleagues, as well as the possibility of using support when faced with challenging situations. The analysis showed that age was not significant for the rating of this support, as opposed to place of residence. Nevertheless, it is worth pointing out that this variable differentiated in a different manner the rating given by the teachers surveyed in 2020 and 2022. A more favourable rating of support of staff involved in inclusive education was found in the group of urban teachers surveyed in 2020. In turn, among the teachers surveyed in 2022, a higher rating of this dimension of support was recorded for teachers employed at rural schools.

Taking into account variables related to occupation and employment, the rating of support of staff involved in inclusive education correlated positively (albeit weakly) with seniority and length of service at the current school, but only among the teachers surveyed in 2020. The type of school they were employed at proved to be an insignificant factor for their ratings in this dimension of support. Regardless of the period in which the teachers were surveyed, the level taught significantly differentiated their rating of support of the staff involved in inclusive education. Teachers working at primary schools covering all levels expressed the highest rating in this respect. They differed significantly in their favourable rating from all the other groups of teachers.

Summarising the aspects of teacher support, it should be emphasised that it constitutes a key element in overcoming resistance to inclusive education. Therefore, in many projects that involve strengthening the idea of quality education for all learners, this support takes many diverse forms taking into account the local context, cultural differences, and the diversified needs of teachers and learners (Sharma, Forlin, Deppeler, & Yang, 2013). The development of a concept to support Polish teachers in relation to the sudden appearance of a large number of learners from refugee families probably requires special involvement on the part of central and local authorities, as well as on the part of researchers working in the field of special and intercultural education.

Chapter 7.
Leadership or collaboration/partnership?
Teachers' point of view

Collaboration in inclusive education as rated by teachers – comparative analysis of 2020 and 2022 study results

A pivotal element of inclusive education aimed at meeting the needs of all learners and taking into account their individual, diverse abilities is the collaboration of all the persons involved in the organisation and provision of this type of education. This collaboration, aimed at pursuing a common goal of each learner achieving the optimum level of their psychosocial and educational development, involves the fulfilment of a variety of roles with complementary competences. Essentially, systematic, dynamic and flexible collaboration between specialists and subject teachers is indicated, with an emphasis placed on the participation of other individuals (including parents) involved in the education process of all learners. In the context of the collaboration of all staff in inclusive education, the question undoubtedly arises about the importance of leaders and leadership, defining the direction, vision and framework of this educational process. The complexity of the organisation and implementation of inclusive education necessitates, as it were, by its very nature the presence of a leadership link determining its structure, course, specificity, and expected functions. In this chapter, we analyse both of these elements of inclusive education: collaboration and the role of leaders from the point of view of the teachers surveyed in 2020 and in 2020, taking into account the sociodemographic variables adopted (gender, age, place of residence) and those related to occupation and employment (job seniority, length of service at the current school, type of school where the teacher is employed, and the level of education taught).

In the first place, we collated collaboration and leadership scores from teachers surveyed in 2020 and 2022. Statistically significant differences were determined in the teachers' ratings (Table 29). Teachers surveyed in 2020 rated collaboration in inclusive education significantly higher, both generally and specifically, compared to teachers surveyed in 2022. Not only was a highly significant variation determined, but a medium effect size was also identified. It is important to emphasise that significant differences between the two groups of teachers were found in the ratings of all specific aspects of collaboration in inclusive education.

Statistically significant differences between the teachers surveyed in 2020 and in 2022 were also found in the case of the rating of leadership in inclusive education (Table 30). Similarly as in the case of the rating of collaboration, statistically higher scores were obtained here by the teachers surveyed in 2020. Significant differences, both in the overall ratings and in the references to specific aspects of leadership, occurred at a level of high statistical significance, and the effect size identified was medium to high. This indicates that the rating of collaboration and leadership in inclusive education by the teachers surveyed in the two periods was radically different, reflected in all the elements considered.

Table 29. Collaboration in inclusive education as rated by the teachers surveyed in 2020 and 2022

Teachers' rating	Teachers surveyed in 2020		Teachers surveyed in 2022		df	t-test	p	Cohen's d
	M	SD	M	SD				
Overall rating								
Collaboration	34.40	3.71	32.99	4.35	6,040	13.63	<0.001	0.650
Specific ratings								
The school provides accessible information to parents and the wider community to promote inclusive education	4.34	0.60	4.13	0.72	6,040	12.14	<0.001	0.742
The school works closely with parents to raise the aspirations and achievements of all learners	4.44	0.59	4.28	0.64	6,040	9.81	<0.001	0.565
The school invites families to discuss issues that are important to them	4.34	0.65	4.18	0.71	6,040	9.45	<0.001	0.557
Input from parents/families is a valued part of the decision-making process and support activities	4.34	0.71	4.17	0.75	6,040	10.38	<0.001	0.592
The school networks with local schools, universities and workplaces to provide a wider range of opportunities for learners	4.33	0.66	4.15	0.69	6,040	10.12	<0.001	0.627
The school collaborates with other entities (e.g., healthcare or welfare facilities) to provide additional support for learners if necessary	4.50	0.59	4.36	0.62	6,040	9.27	<0.001	0.487
All stakeholders are aware of their roles within the school as well as of the roles and contribution of others	4.28	0.72	4.10	0.68	6,040	10.64	<0.001	0.627
External stakeholders/partners participate in the process of the school's assessment and/or self-assessment	3.82	0.65	3.62	0.69	6,040	13.63	<0.001	0.696

M – arithmetic mean; SD – standard deviation; t – Student's t-test for independent data

Table 30. Leadership in inclusive education as rated by the teachers surveyed in 2020 and 2022

Teachers' rating	Teachers surveyed in 2020		Teachers surveyed in 2022		df	t-test	p	Cohen's d
	M	SD	M	SD				
Overall rating								
Leadership	52.55	5.21	49.71	7.16	6,040	17.76	<0.001	0.885
Specific ratings								
Leaders use a collaborative process to develop a shared vision and values that foster inclusion	4.50	0.52	4.26	0.71	6,040	15.32	<0.001	0.835
Leaders support strong relationships based on trust	4.54	0.77	4.26	0.73	6,040	16.75	<0.001	0.901
Leaders facilitate effective communication between all stakeholders (e.g., staff, learners, parents, other professionals, community members)	4.53	0.66	4.28	0.72	6,040		<0.001	0.870
Leaders actively manage change and dealing with uncertainty/unknowns	4.31	0.63	4.08	0.67	6,040	15.91	<0.001	0.801
Leaders engage all stakeholders in the decision-making process	4.22	0.59	4.00	0.64	6,040	14.06	<0.001	0.731
Leaders develop a climate in which all learners are known and treated as individuals	4.36	0.77	4.13	0.76	6,040	11.88	<0.001	0.800
Leaders perceive inclusion as a key value for the improvement of the quality of work at school	4.45	0.72	4.15	0.81	6,040	13.90	<0.001	1.011
Leaders collect and use data to monitor and evaluate practice and its impact on all learners	4.37	0.55	4.17	0.61	6,040	17.85	<0.001	0.696
Leaders use research evidence to plan and implement improvements	4.36	0.73	4.13	0.69	6,040	12.20	<0.001	0.801
Leaders focus on learning to raise the aspirations and achievements of all learners	4.28	0.64	4.06	0.70	6,040	14.40	<0.001	0.766
Leaders operate in such a way as to make sure that all stakeholders understand the assessment processes used at school and the way in which such information can be used (e.g., formative assessment for learning)	4.23	0.67	4.01	0.70	6,040	13.41	<0.001	0.750

Table 30 *(Continued)*

Teachers' rating	Teachers surveyed in 2020		Teachers surveyed in 2022		df	t-test	p	Cohen's d
	M	SD	M	SD				
Leaders monitor equal access to full activity and engagement in the learning process and participation in school activities	4.40	0.72	4.19	0.69	6,040	13.39	<0.001	0.731

M – arithmetic mean; SD – standard deviation; t – Student's t-test for independent data

Collaboration and leadership as rated by teachers surveyed in 2020 – importance of sociodemographic as well as job- and employment-related variables

The analysis of collaboration and leadership in the context of the sociodemographic as well as job- and employment-related variables adopted will be preceded by a collation of the scores in both of these elements of inclusive education. To compare the results in terms of collaboration and leadership, we divided them by the number of items. An analysis using Student's t-test for dependent data showed statistically significant differences in the teachers' ratings. Leadership was rated significantly higher than collaboration ($M_{leadership}$=4.40, SD=0.43, $M_{collaboration}$=4.30, SD=0.46, T=12.74, p<0.001). The gender of the teachers surveyed in 2020 significantly differentiated their ratings of both collaboration and leadership in inclusive education. The results obtained in this area are presented in Tables 31 and 32. Female teachers rated both collaboration and leadership in inclusive education significantly higher compared to male teachers. This variation was noticeable in the overall rating of both of these elements of inclusive education, as well as with regard to the specific aspects.

Correlation analysis showed that the age of the teachers surveyed in 2020 was not statistically significantly linked to the rating of either collaboration (r=-0.021, p=0.243) or leadership (r=-0.019, p=0.296) in inclusive education. In turn, the last sociodemographic variable taken into account, i. e. place of residence, was found to significantly differentiate the teachers' rating of collaboration and leadership in inclusive education. The results obtained in this area are presented in Tables 33 and 34. In terms of the rating of collaboration in inclusive education, teachers from urban areas scored significantly higher than teachers from rural areas, with a small effect size found. Urban teachers rated the following levels of this collaboration significantly higher: working with parents to raise the achievements and aspirations of all learners, discussions with parents on aspects of importance to them, and recognising the parents' contribution to the decision-making process and support activities. In terms of the rating of leadership in inclusive education, urban teachers also scored significantly higher than rural teachers. They obtained significantly higher results both in the overall rating and in relation to certain specific aspects of leadership: expressed in the development of a shared vision and values that foster inclusion, leaders' active attitude with regard to managing change and uncertainty, leaders monitoring equal access to full activity and engagement in the learning process as well as participation in school activities.

Table 31. Impact of teachers' gender on the rating of collaboration by the teachers surveyed in 2020

Teachers' rating	Female teachers		Male teachers		df	U-test	p
	M	SD	M	SD			
Overall rating							
Collaboration	34.51	3.73	33.92	3.58	3,186	3.44	0.001
Specific ratings							
The school provides accessible information to parents and the wider community to promote inclusive education	3.84	0.76	3.82	0.67	3,186	0.51	0.610
The school works closely with parents to raise the aspirations and achievements of all learners	4.30	0.65	4.21	0.62	3,186	3.25	0.001
The school invites families to discuss issues that are important to them	4.51	0.67	4.46	0.61	3,186	1.91	0.056
Input from parents/families is a valued part of the decision-making process and support activities	4.33	0.79	4.31	0.81	3,186	0.88	0.385
The school networks with local schools, universities and workplaces to provide a wider range of opportunities for learners	4.37	0.88	4.23	0.78	3,186	4.85	<0.001
The school collaborates with other entities (e.g., healthcare or welfare facilities) to provide additional support for learners if necessary	4.37	0.90	4.24	0.87	3,186	4.33	<0.001
All stakeholders are aware of their roles within the school as well as of the roles and contribution of others	4.45	0.69	4.38	0.70	3,186	2.68	0.007
External stakeholders/partners participate in the process of the school's assessment and/or self-assessment	4.45	0.66	4.28	0.61	3,186	2.45	0.014

M – arithmetic mean; SD – standard deviation; U – Mann-Whitney U-test

Table 32. Impact of teachers' gender on the rating of leadership by the teachers surveyed in 2020

Teachers' rating	Female teachers		Male teachers		df	U-test	p
	M	SD	M	SD			
Overall rating							
Leadership	52.68	5.22	51.95	5.13	3,186	3.05	0.002
Specific ratings							
Leaders use a collaborative process to develop a shared vision and values that foster inclusion	4.51	0.78	4.48	0.81	3,186	1.14	0.252
Leaders support strong relationships based on trust	4.54	0.66	4.53	0.59	3,186	0.66	0.511
Leaders facilitate effective communication between all stakeholders (e.g., staff, learners, parents, other professionals, community members)	4.54	0.59	4.50	0.64	3,186	1.35	0.177
Leaders actively manage change and dealing with uncertainty/unknowns	4.33	0.75	4.24	0.73	3,186	3.21	0.001
Leaders engage all stakeholders in the decision-making process	4.23	0.68	4.14	0.72	3,186	3.29	0.001
Leaders develop a climate in which all learners are known and treated as individuals	4.38	0.65	4.27	0.61	3,186	4.28	<0.001
Leaders perceive inclusion as a key value for the improvement of the quality of work at school	4.47	0.53	4.38	0.66	3,186	3.37	0.001
Leaders collect and use data to monitor and evaluate practice and its impact on all learners	4.37	0.69	4.32	0.72	3,186	2.11	0.034
Leaders use research evidence to plan and implement improvements	4.37	0.76	4.32	0.72	3,186	3.47	0.030
Leaders focus on learning to raise the aspirations and achievements of all learners	4.30	0.69	4.21	0.71	3,186	0.80	0.001
Leaders operate in such a way as to make sure that all stakeholders understand the assessment processes used at school and the way in which such information can be used (e.g., formative assessment for learning)	4.23	0.63	4.21	0.77	3,186	2.07	0.422
Leaders monitor equal access to full activity and engagement in the learning process as well as participation in school activities	4.41	0.73	4.36	0.67	3,186	3.05	0.038

M – arithmetic mean; SD – standard deviation; U – Mann-Whitney U-test

Table 33. Impact of teachers' place of residence on the rating of collaboration in inclusive education by the teachers surveyed in 2020

Teachers' rating	Urban teachers		Rural teachers		df	t-test	p	Cohen's d
	M	SD	M	SD				
Overall rating								
Collaboration	34.53	3.81	34.19	3.53	3,186	2.51	0.012	0.196
Specific ratings								
The school provides accessible information to parents and the wider community to promote inclusive education	3.84	0.77	3.82	0.74	3,186	0.89	0.371	–
The school works closely with parents to raise the aspirations and achievements of all learners	4.30	0.74	4.24	0.70	3,186	2.69	0.008	0.217
The school invites families to discuss issues that are important to them	4.51	0.89	4.45	0.86	3,186	2.16	0.031	0.228
Input from parents/families is a valued part of the decision-making process and support activities	4.37	0.67	4.26	0.70	3,186	4.79	<0.001	0.419
The school networks with local schools, universities and workplaces to provide a wider range of opportunities for learners	4.35	0.59	4.33	0.62	3,186	1.17	0.243	–
The school collaborates with other entities (e.g., healthcare or welfare facilities) to provide additional support for learners if necessary	4.36	0.71	4.32	0.68	3,186	1.66	0.096	–
All stakeholders are aware of their roles within the school as well as of the roles and contribution of others	4.44	0.66	4.43	0.69	3,186	-0.11	0.912	–
External stakeholders/partners participate in the process of the school's assessment and/or self-assessment	4.35	0.72	4.31	0.70	3,186	1.81	0.070	–

M – arithmetic mean; SD – standard deviation; t – Student's t-test for independent data

Table 34. Impact of teachers' place of residence on the rating of leadership in inclusive education by the teachers surveyed in 2020

Teachers' rating	Urban teachers		Rural teachers		df	t-test	p	Cohen's d
	M	SD	M	SD				
Overall rating								
Leadership	52.80	5.27	52.14	5.08	3,186	3.44	0.001	0.245
Specific ratings								
Leaders use a collaborative process to develop a shared vision and values that foster inclusion	4.62	0.59	4.50	0.62	3,186	1.44	0.001	0.456
Leaders support strong relationships based on trust	4.35	0.55	4.33	0.58	3,186	0.93	0.148	-
Leaders facilitate effective communication between all stakeholders (e.g., staff, learners, parents, other professionals, community members)	4.57	0.76	4.54	0.79	3,186	1.60	0.110	-
Leaders actively manage change and dealing with uncertainty/unknowns	4.60	0.82	4.55	0.88	3,186	1.75	0.041	0.190
Leaders engage all stakeholders in the decision-making process	4.60	0.56	4.57	0.61	3,186	1.17	0.241	-
Leaders develop a climate in which all learners are known and treated as individuals	4.26	0.66	4.24	0.70	3,186	0.91	0.362	-
Leaders perceive inclusion as a key value for the improvement of the quality of work at school	4.28	0.67	4.26	0.69	3,186	1.06	0.291	-
Leaders collect and use data to monitor and evaluate practice and its impact on all learners	4.47	0.72	4.45	0.73	3,186	1.16	0.248	-
Leaders use research evidence to plan and implement improvements	4.48	0.77	4.47	0.80	3,186	0.08	0.935	-
Leaders focus on learning to raise the aspirations and achievements of all learners	4.33	0.66	4.25	0.68	3,186	1.64	0.031	-
Leaders operate in such a way as to make sure that all stakeholders understand the assessment processes used at school and the way in which such information can be used (e.g., formative assessment for learning)	4.62	0.69	4.61	0.71	3,186	0.57	0.567	-

Table 34 *(Continued)*

Teachers' rating	Urban teachers		Rural teachers		df	t-test	p	Cohen's d
	M	SD	M	SD				
Leaders monitor equal access to full activity and engagement in the learning process as well as participation in school activities	4.51	0.72	4.41	0.74	3,186	1.95	0.041	0.380

M – arithmetic mean; SD – standard deviation; t – Student's t-test for independent data

An analysis of the rating of collaboration and leadership in inclusive education by the teachers surveyed in 2020, taking into account job- and employment-related variables, yielded the results described below. Job seniority did not correlate statistically significantly with the rating of either collaboration or leadership in inclusive education (r=0.002, p=0.914; r=0.014, p=0.428, respectively). No statistically significant correlations were found between the teachers' length of service at their current place of employment and their rating of collaboration and leadership (r=0.024, p=0.184; r=-0.012, p=0.504, respectively). The type of school where the teachers were employed did not significantly differentiate their rating of leadership in inclusive education ($M_{\text{state school teachers}}$=52.60; SD=5.20; $M_{\text{non-state school teachers}}$=52.05; SD=5.26; Mann-Whitney U=1.82; p=0.069). In turn, when it came to rating collaboration in inclusive education, the type of school where the teachers were employed proved to be a significantly differentiating variable. The results obtained in this area are presented in Table 35.

State school teachers rated collaboration in inclusive education significantly higher compared to non-state school teachers. They also scored significantly higher in their ratings of specific aspects of collaboration: the school's networking with local schools, universities and workplaces to provide more opportunities for all learners, the school's collaboration with other significant entities to provide additional support to learners when needed, the participation of external partners in the school's assessment or self-assessment process. The level of education taught also proved to be a significantly differentiating factor in their rating of collaboration in inclusive education, as well as of leadership. The results obtained in this area are presented in Tables 36 and 37.

Table 35. Impact of the school type (state/non-state) on the rating of collaboration in inclusive education among the teachers surveyed in 2020

Teachers' rating	State school teachers		Non-state school teachers		df	U-test	p
	M	SD	M	SD			
Overall rating							
Collaboration	34.47	3.67	33.84	4.01	3,186	2.83	0.005
Specific ratings							
The school provides accessible information to parents and the wider community to promote inclusive education	4.34	0.76	4.30	0.68	3,186	1.05	0.294
The school works closely with parents to raise the aspirations and achievements of all learners	4.44	0.72	4.40	0.70	3,186	1.30	0.193
The school invites families to discuss issues that are important to them	4.35	0.59	4.32	0.61	3,186	0.66	0.505
Input from parents/families is a valued part of the decision-making process and support activities	4.35	0.62	4.28	0.66	3,186	1.81	0.070
The school networks with local schools, universities and workplaces to provide a wider range of opportunities for learners	4.34	0.67	4.20	0.70	3,186	4.01	<0.001
The school collaborates with other entities (e.g., healthcare or welfare facilities) to provide additional support for learners if necessary	4.51	0.72	4.37	0.77	3,186	4.53	<0.001
All stakeholders are aware of their roles within the school as well as of the roles and contribution of others	4.28	0.66	4.31	0.69	3,186	-0.84	0.398
External stakeholders/partners participate in the process of the school's assessment and/or self-assessment	4.85	0.59	4.67	0.61	3,186	4.14	<0.001

M – arithmetic mean; SD – standard deviation; U – Mann-Whitney U-test

Table 36. Impact of the level taught on the rating of collaboration in inclusive education among the teachers surveyed in 2020

Rating	Pre-school teachers (1)		Teachers of primary school levels 1 to 3 (2)		Teachers of primary school levels 4 to 8 (3)		Teachers of all primary school levels (4)		Secondary school teachers (5)		One-way ANOVA		
	M	SD	M	SD	M	SD	M	SD	M	SD	F	Inter-group comparison	p
Overall rating													
Collaboration	34.74	3.83	34.21	3.52	35.50	4.21	34.28	3.54	34.30	3.60	2.64*	1–4 1–5	0.004 0.019
Specific ratings													
1	4.38	0.59	4.35	0.60	4.63	0.56	4.32	0.58	4.31	0.61	2.15	–	
2	4.49	0.70	4.48	0.69	4.75	0.71	4.45	0.72	4.35	0.68	6.34***	1–4 1–5	0.018 0.032
3	4.42	0.64	4.36	0.66	4.50	0.69	4.35	0.70	4.23	0.72	8.64***	1–5 2–5 4–5	<0.001 0.002 <0.001
4	4.42	0.69	4.37	0.70	4.38	0.67	4.35	0.71	4.24	0.69	8.41***	1–4 1–5 2–5 4–5	0.018 <0.001 0.012 0.001
5	4.36	0.77	4.19	0.76	4.38	0.69	4.26	0.80	4.47	0.81	16.47***	1–4 1–5 2–5 4–5	0.010 <0.001 0.008 <0.001
6	4.48	0.55	4.45	0.57	4.75	0.60	4.50	0.61	4.53	0.64	1.58	–	

Table 36 (Continued)

Rating	Pre-school teachers (1)		Teachers of primary school levels 1 to 3 (2)		Teachers of primary school levels 4 to 8 (3)		Teachers of all primary school levels (4)		Secondary school teachers (5)		One-way ANOVA		
	M	SD	M	SD	M	SD	M	SD	M	SD	F	Inter-group comparison	p
7	4.33	0.66	4.31	0.67	4.25	0.73	4.25	0.76	4.29	0.77	2.86*	1–4	0.001
8	3.88	0.66	3.69	0.70	3.88	0.72	3.81	0.75	3.89	0.69	3.74*	2–4 2–5 4–5	0.046 0.001 0.021

1: The school provides accessible information to parents and the wider community to promote inclusive education; 2: The school works closely with parents to raise the aspirations and achievements of all learners; 3: The school invites families to discuss issues that are important to them; 4: Input from parents/families is a valued part of the decision-making process and support activities; 5: The school networks with local schools, universities and workplaces to provide a wider range of opportunities for learners; 6: The school collaborates with other entities (e.g., healthcare or welfare facilities) to provide additional support for learners if necessary; 7: All stakeholders are aware of their roles within the school as well as of the roles and contribution of others; 8: External stakeholders/partners participate in the process of the school's assessment and/or self-assessment

Pre-school teachers rated collaboration in inclusive education significantly higher compared to teachers of all primary school levels and secondary school teachers. A significant variation between the groups of teachers surveyed in 2020 was found in the rating of many specific aspects of collaboration, except those related to the school providing information aimed at promoting inclusive education to parents and the wider community, and the school's collaboration with other entities to provide additional support to learners as required. Pre-school teachers, as compared to teachers of all primary school levels and secondary school teachers, scored significantly higher in relation to the following areas of collaboration: working with parents to raise the aspirations and achievements of all learners; discussing issues of importance with parents; parents' participation in the decision-making process and support activities; and the school networking with local schools, universities or workplaces providing wider opportunities for learners. It is worth emphasising that secondary school teachers, compared to teachers of primary school levels 1 to 3 and of all primary school levels, rated significantly lower areas of collaboration in inclusive education related to: parents' participation in discussions on issues of importance to them, in the decision-making process and in the development of support activities; the school networking with other local institutions that can provide learners with an extended range of opportunities; and the participation of external stakeholders in the process of assessment and/or self-assessment of the school's work.

In their rating of leadership in inclusive education, teachers surveyed in 2020 working at different levels of education, in contrast to the rating of collaboration, agreed to more extent with regard to the specific opinions expressed. The highest overall rating was given by pre-school teachers, significantly higher compared to that expressed by teachers of all primary school levels and secondary school teachers. Pre-school teachers also rated highest leadership in inclusive education expressed in leaders' activity in managing change and dealing with uncertain situations, significantly higher compared to teachers of all primary school levels. In their rating of the following aspects of leadership: leaders engaging all stakeholders involved in inclusive education in the decision-making process, and leaders' active contribution to the development of a school climate in which all learners are known and treated as individuals, teachers of all primary school levels and secondary school teachers scored significantly lower than pre-school teachers. The greatest variation between the groups of teachers was found in the rating of leadership manifesting itself in leaders' focus on the learning process, oriented towards raising the aspirations and achievements of all learners. Primary school teachers of levels 4 to 8 rated this aspect of leadership the highest. These teachers and pre-school teachers scored significantly higher in this respect compared to teachers of all primary school levels and secondary school teachers.

Table 37. Impact of the level taught on the rating of leadership in inclusive education by the teachers surveyed in 2020

Rating	Pre-school teachers (1)		Teachers of primary school levels 1 to 3 (2)		Teachers of primary school levels 4 to 8 (3)		Teachers of all primary school levels (4)		Secondary school teachers (5)		One-way ANOVA		
	M	SD	M	SD	M	SD	M	SD	M	SD	F	Inter-group comparison	p
Overall rating													
Leadership	52.97	5.27	52.52	5.40	55.87	5.00	52.37	5.88	52.39	5.34	2.80*	1–4 1–5	0.007 0.031
Specific ratings													
1	4.53	0.53	4.47	0.50	4.63	0.51	4.49	0.54	4.50	0.52	1.15	–	
2	4.56	0.59	4.53	0.55	4.75	0.54	4.53	0.56	4.53	0.58	0.81	–	
3	4.56	0.60	4.51	0.57	4.63	0.55	4.52	0.52	4.53	0.60	1.08	–	
4	4.36	0.57	4.32	0.54	4.63	0.55	4.28	0.51	4.31	0.57	3.09*	1–4	0.002
5	4.29	0.62	4.24	0.59	4.63	0.57	4.17	0.59	4.20	0.61	5.83***	1–4 1–5 3–4	<0.001 0.006 0.041
6	4.41	0.54	4.34	0.57	4.50	0.55	4.35	0.60	4.33	0.57	2.67*	1–4 1–5	0.009 0.004
7	4.49	0.62	4.46	0.59	4.75	0.57	4.45	0.55	4.41	0.59	2.37	–	
8	4.40	0.55	4.36	0.56	4.63	0.60	4.35	0.59	4.35	0.55	1–36		
9	4.40	0.57	4.35	0.58	4.75	0.54	4.35	0.55	4.35	0.58	2–18	–	

Table 37 (Continued)

Rating	Pre-school teachers (1) M	SD	Teachers of primary school levels 1 to 3 (2) M	SD	Teachers of primary school levels 4 to 8 (3) M	SD	Teachers of all primary school levels (4) M	SD	Secondary school teachers (5) M	SD	One-way ANOVA F	Inter-group comparison	p
10	4.32	0.58	4.29	0.60	4.88	0.55	4.27	0.57	4.26	0.59	3–73**	1–3 1–4 1–5 2–3 3–4 3–5	0.007 0.028 0.026 0.005 0.003 0.003
11	4.24	0.53	4.25	0.54	4.50	0.55	4.21	0.60	4.23	0.54	0.74	–	
12	4.41	0.55	4.38	0.57	4.63	0.59	4.39	0.54	4.39	0.58	0.71	–	

1: Leaders use a collaborative process to develop a shared vision and values that foster inclusion; 2: Leaders support strong relationships based on trust; 3: Leaders facilitate effective communication between all stakeholders (e.g., staff, learners, parents, other professionals, community members); 4: Leaders actively manage change and dealing with uncertainty/unknowns; 5: Leaders engage all stakeholders in the decision-making process; 6: Leaders develop a climate in which all learners are known and treated as individuals; 7: Leaders perceive inclusion as a key value for the improvement of the quality of work at school; 8: Leaders collect and use data to monitor and evaluate practice and its impact on all learners; 9: Leaders use research evidence to plan and implement improvements; 10: Leaders focus on learning to raise the aspirations and achievements of all learners; 11: Leaders operate in such a way as to make sure that all stakeholders understand the assessment processes used at school and the way in which such information can be used (e.g., formative assessment for learning); 12: Leaders monitor equal access to full activity and engagement in the learning process as well as participation in school activities

Collaboration and leadership as rated by the teachers surveyed in 2022 – importance of sociodemographic as well as job- and employment-related variables

The remaining part of this chapter contains an analysis of the results concerning collaboration and leadership in inclusive education among the teachers surveyed in 2022. Firstly, we compare the ratings of collaboration and leadership using Student's t-test for dependent data. The results indicate that this group of teachers rated leadership significantly higher than collaboration in inclusive education ($M_{leadership}$=4.34, SD=0.55, $M_{collaboration}$=4.19, SD=0.59, T=13.01, p<0.001). We performed subsequent analyses taking into account sociodemographic as well as job- and employment-related variables. Teachers' gender was found to be a factor that did not statistically significantly differentiate either their rating of collaboration in inclusive education ($M_{female\ teachers}$=33.02, SD=4.33, $M_{male\ teachers}$=32.78, SD=4.78, Mann-Whitney U=1.18, p=0.317) or their rating of leadership in inclusive education ($M_{female\ teachers}$=49.67, SD=7.23, $M_{male\ teachers}$=49.97, SD=6.75, Mann-Whitney U=-0.79, p=0.431). The teachers' age correlated statistically significantly and positively (albeit weakly) with leadership ratings (r=0.171, p<0.001), whereas no significant correlation was found between age and the rating of collaboration in inclusive education (r=0.006, p=0.541). Higher leadership ratings were correlated with older age among teachers. Place of residence was another factor that did not differentiate in a statistically significant manner either the rating of collaboration in inclusive education ($M_{urban\ teachers}$=32.96, SD=4.50, $M_{rural\ teachers}$=33.05, t=-0.55, p=0.585), or the rating of leadership in inclusive education ($M_{urban\ teachers}$=49.55, SD=7.55, $M_{rural\ teachers}$=49.97, t=-1.52, p=0.127).

Teachers' job seniority correlated significantly and positively with both their rating of collaboration in inclusive education (r=0.111, p=0.004) and their rating of leadership (r=0.152, p<0.001). The correlations that were found point to weak associations between these variables, revealing that higher ratings of collaboration and leadership in inclusive education are associated with longer job seniority among teachers. Positive and also weak relationships were found between length of service at the teachers' current place of employment and their rating of collaboration (r=0.183, p<0.001) and leadership (r=0.167, p<0.001) in inclusive education. Higher ratings for collaboration and leadership are associated with longer length of service at the current school among the teachers surveyed in 2022. Another variable taken into account, namely the type of school where the teachers were employed, was found to be a factor that did not differentiate in a statistically significant manner the rating of leadership in inclusive education in this group of teachers ($M_{state\ school\ teachers}$=33.01; SD=4.32; $M_{non-state\ school\ teachers}$=32.58;

SD=4.85; Mann-Whitney U=1.13; p=0.259). The type of school where the teachers were employed did not significantly differentiate their rating of leadership in inclusive education either ($M_{\text{state school teachers}}$=49.70; SD=7.14; $M_{\text{non-state school teachers}}$=49.95; SD=7.67; Mann-Whitney U=-0.40; p=0.689). In turn, the level taught proved to be a variable differentiating the rating of collaboration and leadership in inclusive education in this group of teachers. The results obtained in this area are presented in Tables 38 and 39.

Teachers of all primary school levels rated collaboration in inclusive education highest compared to pre-school, primary school levels 1 to 3 and primary school levels 4 to 8 teachers. A significant variation was also found between the teacher groups in the rating of four out of the eight specific areas of collaboration in inclusive education. With regard to the collaborative aspect involving the school inviting parents to discuss issues of importance to them, teachers of all primary school levels scored highest, differing statistically significantly from all other teacher groups in this respect. In terms of recognising the contribution of families to the decision-making process and support activities, these teachers also gave the highest rating, significantly higher than pre-school, primary school levels 4 to 8, and secondary school teachers. In terms of collaboration in the form of the school networking with local schools, universities and workplaces to broaden opportunities for learners, the highest rating was given by secondary school teachers, significantly higher compared to all the other teacher groups. In turn, the school's collaboration with other entities to provide additional support for learners was rated highest by teachers of all primary school levels, significantly higher compared to pre-school, primary school levels 1 to 3 and primary school levels 4 to 8 teachers.

It is worth emphasising that a greater differentiation between groups of teachers differing in terms of the level taught was marked in the rating of leadership in inclusive education. Teachers of all primary school levels expressed the highest rating, significantly higher than primary school levels 1 to 3, primary school levels 4 to 8, and secondary school teachers. In the vast majority of leadership areas, teachers' ratings varied significantly. In the rating of leaders using the collaborative process to develop a shared vision and values promoting inclusion, teachers of primary school levels 1 to 3 scored lowest, significantly lower than pre-school, all primary school levels and secondary school teachers. Leaders recognising collaboration as support for strong and trusted relationships is most characteristic of teachers of all primary school levels, compared to primary school levels 1 to 3, primary school levels 4 to 8, and secondary school teachers. Pre-school teachers also rated this leadership aspect much higher compared to the aforementioned groups of teachers. Similar results were found with regard to the rating concerning leadership involving the leaders facilitating effective communication between all stakeholders involved in inclusive education. Primary school levels 1 to 3 teachers were found to rate leaders' activity in managing change and dealing with uncertain situations lowest, significantly lower than pre-school, all primary school levels, and secondary school teachers. Teachers rated the activity of leaders aimed at engaging all stakeholders in the decision-making process in a similar manner. The highest rating of leaders' development of a school climate conducive to getting to know each learner and treating them as individuals was found among pre-school and all primary school levels teachers, who differed significantly in this respect from the other groups of teachers. Leadership in the form of leaders recognising inclusion as a key value determining the improvement of the school's work was rated highest by teachers of all primary school levels, significantly higher than by primary school levels 1 to 3, primary school levels 4 to 8, and secondary school teachers. This group of teachers also rated particularly highly leadership expressed in the leaders monitoring equal access to full participation in the learning process and in the school activities offered, much higher compared to primary school levels 1 to 3 and primary school levels 4 to 8 teachers. In turn, leadership perceived as leaders using scientific research to plan improvements to the teaching process was rated highest by pre-school and all primary school levels teachers, significantly higher than by primary school levels 1 to 3 and primary school levels 4 to 8 teachers.

Table 38. Impact of the level taught on the rating of collaboration in inclusive education by the teachers surveyed in 2022

Rating	Pre-school teachers (1)		Teachers of primary school levels 1 to 3 (2)		Teachers of primary school levels 4 to 8 (3)		Teachers of all primary school levels (4)		Secondary school teachers (5)		One-way ANOVA		
	M	SD	M	SD	M	SD	M	SD	M	SD	F	Inter-group comparison	p
Collaboration						Overall rating							
	32.78	4.85	32.64	4.42	32.80	4.30	33.33	4.01	33.15	4.31	2.81*	1-4 2-4 3-4	0.031 0.004 0.040
						Specific ratings							
1	4.11	0.74	4.08	0.76	4.13	0.70	4.15	0.71	4.16	0.74	1.17	–	
2	4.26	0.68	4.27	0.70	4.27	0.74	4.33	0.72	4.24	0.69	2.10	–	
3	4.17	0.70	4.15	0.73	4.16	0.66	4.27	0.64	4.12	0.70	4.40**	1-4 2-4 3-4 4-5	0.016 0.006 0.009 <0.001
4	4.19	0.68	4.12	0.70	4.14	0.72	4.23	0.66	4.11	0.68	3.37**	2-4 3-4 4-5	0.007 0.022 0.002
5	4.13	0.72	4.07	0.71	4.08	0.68	4.16	0.67	4.32	0.60	10.68***	1-5 2-4 2-5 3-4 3-5 4-5	<0.001 0.026 <0.001 0.049 <0.001 <0.001

Table 38 *(Continued)*

Rating	Pre-school teachers (1)		Teachers of primary school levels 1 to 3 (2)		Teachers of primary school levels 4 to 8 (3)		Teachers of all primary school levels (4)		Secondary school teachers (5)		One-way ANOVA		
	M	SD	M	SD	M	SD	M	SD	M	SD	F	Inter-group comparison	p
6	4.27	0.73	4.33	0.70	4.33	0.69	4.42	0.68	4.39	0.72	5.47***	1–4 1–5 2–4 3–4	<0.001 0.001 0.011 0.015
7	4.09	0.68	4.04	0.67	4.08	0.71	4.15	0.72	4.12	0.70	1.93	–	
8	3.58	0.70	3.58	0.72	3.61	0.68	3.63	0.70	3.69	0.67	1.75	–	

1: The school provides accessible information to parents and the wider community to promote inclusive education; 2: The school works closely with parents to raise the aspirations and achievements of all learners; 3: The school invites families to discuss issues that are important to them; 4: Input from parents/families is a valued part of the decision-making process and support activities; 5: The school networks with local schools, universities and workplaces to provide a wider range of opportunities for learners; 6: The school collaborates with other entities (e.g., healthcare or welfare facilities) to provide additional support for learners if necessary; 7: All stakeholders are aware of their roles within the school as well as of the roles and contribution of others; 8: External stakeholders/partners participate in the process of the school's assessment and/or self-assessment

Table 39. Impact of the level taught on the rating of leadership in inclusive education by the teachers surveyed in 2022

Rating	Pre-school teachers (1)		Teachers of primary school levels 1 to 3 (2)		Teachers of primary school levels 4 to 8 (3)		Teachers of all primary school levels (4)		Secondary school teachers (5)		One-way ANOVA		
	M	SD	M	SD	M	SD	M	SD	M	SD	F	Inter-group comparison	p
Overall rating													
Leadership	50.28	7.36	48.76	7.33	49.04	7.54	50.52	6.24	49.51	7.64	6.97***	1-2 1-3 2-4 3-4 4-5	0.001 0.007 <0.001 <0.001 0.010
Specific ratings													
1	4.31	0.73	4.15	0.76	4.21	0.72	4.32	0.65	4.27	0.76	5.29***	1-2 1-3 2-4 2-5 3-4	0.001 0.031 <0.001 0.010 0.007
2	4.34	0.72	4.13	0.75	4.17	0.65	4.38	0.69	4.23	0.70	12.58***	1-2 1-3 1-5 2-4 2-5 3-4 4-5	<0.001 <0.001 0.018 <0.001 0.032 <0.001 <0.001

Table 39 (Continued)

Rating	Pre-school teachers (1)		Teachers of primary school levels 1 to 3 (2)		Teachers of primary school levels 4 to 8 (3)		Teachers of all primary school levels (4)		Secondary school teachers (5)		One-way ANOVA		
	M	SD	M	SD	M	SD	M	SD	M	SD	F	Inter-group comparison	p
3	4.34	0.69	4.17	0.71	4.18	0.67	4.38	0.70	4.23	0.65	11.30***	1–2 1–3 2–4 3–4 4–5	<0.001 <0.001 <0.001 <0.001 0.001
4	4.11	0.75	3.98	0.70	4.03	0.67	4.13	0.73	4.10	0.69	4.73**	1–2 2–4 2–5 3–4	0.004 <0.001 0.005 0.008
5	4.10	0.66	3.90	0.73	3.96	0.68	4.07	0.72	3.96	0.74	6.70***	1–2 1–3 1–5 2–4 3–4 4–5	<0.001 0.004 0.003 <0.001 0.008 0.006
6	4.20	0.74	4.02	0.69	4.07	0.72	4.22	0.65	4.07	0.70	9.07***	1–2 1–3 1–5 2–4 3–4 4–5	<0.001 0.006 0.006 <0.001 <0.001 <0.001

Table 39 *(Continued)*

Rating	Pre-school teachers (1)		Teachers of primary school levels 1 to 3 (2)		Teachers of primary school levels 4 to 8 (3)		Teachers of all primary school levels (4)		Secondary school teachers (5)		One-way ANOVA		
	M	SD	M	SD	M	SD	M	SD	M	SD	F	Inter-group comparison	p
7	4.17	0.80	4.09	0.78	4.09	0.76	4.23	0.73	4.10	0.76	4.06**	2–4 3–4 4–5	0.004 0.002 0.004
8	4.20	0.75	4.13	0.70	4.13	0.65	4.19	0.68	4.18	0.70	1.44	–	
9	4.18	0.73	4.07	0.71	4.06	0.68	4.18	0.66	4.11	0.65	3.63**	1–2 1–3 2–4 3–4	0.017 0.014 0.005 0.004
10	4.09	0.66	4.03	0.71	4.01	0.73	4.11	0.69	4.06	0.68	2.06	–	
11	4.03	0.74	3.96	0.70	3.99	0.72	4.06	0.70	3.99	0.69	2.12	–	
12	4.21	0.62	4.13	0.69	4.14	0.70	4.25	0.72	4.19	0.74	3.59**	2–4 3–4	0.001 0.003

1: Leaders use a collaborative process to develop a shared vision and values that foster inclusion; 2: Leaders support strong relationships based on trust; 3: Leaders facilitate effective communication between all stakeholders (e.g., staff, learners, parents, other professionals, community members); 4: Leaders actively manage change and dealing with uncertainty/unknowns; 5: Leaders engage all stakeholders in the decision-making process; 6: Leaders develop a climate in which all learners are known and treated as individuals; 7: Leaders perceive inclusion as a key value for the improvement of the quality of work at school; 8: Leaders collect and use data to monitor and evaluate practice and its impact on all learners; 9: Leaders use research evidence to plan and implement improvements; 10: Leaders focus on learning to raise the aspirations and achievements of all learners; 11: Leaders operate in such a way as to make sure that all stakeholders understand the assessment processes used at school and the way in which such information can be used (e.g., formative assessment for learning); 12: Leaders monitor equal access to full activity and engagement in the learning process as well as participation in school activities

Conclusion and discussion

Summarising the results of the analyses performed with regard to the teachers' rating of collaboration and leadership in inclusive education, emphasis is found to have been placed mainly on the role of leadership, and to a smaller extent on the role of collaboration. A tendency to express such ratings characterised the teachers surveyed in both periods under consideration. The higher rating of leadership by teachers may therefore indicate not only the vital importance of leadership in inclusive education, but also the expressed expectations of teachers concerning the presence of leaders, guiding their actions and supporting the ongoing process of teaching of all learners. The emphasis placed on the importance of leadership probably reflects the teachers' perceived need to build a concrete and clear vision for the school and well-defined educational solutions – in this case with regard to inclusive education and teaching. Leadership is, on the one hand, about setting the direction, developing a vision for the school's future, as well as orienting people's actions. On the other hand, it is also about motivating and inspiring as well as releasing energy in people (Wiśniewska, 2016). The high importance attributed to leadership in Polish schools may also be associated with the lack of a legally sanctioned position of Special Educational Needs Coordinators (SENCor) present in many education systems in other countries (Farrell, 1998; Mackenzie, 2007; Tissot, 2013). Important SENCor tasks include primarily those inherent in the leadership role, including coordinating activities for learners with special educational needs (SEN), advising teachers, defining the strategic development of the school's policy with regard to learners' special needs, looking after the records of learners with SEN, or managing learning support assistants (MacBeath et al., 2006; Mackenzie, 2007; Tissot, 2013). Arguably, the teachers surveyed, while emphasising the importance of leadership, were at the same time expressing an expectation of support in the areas mentioned.

In turn, the significantly lower rating of collaboration in inclusive education may reflect the actual problems of the staff participating in this type of education at the level of joint implementation of tasks that involve (or should involve) different groups of people: specialists, parents, etc. In this context, it is worth mentioning that collaboration (cooperation) is attributed an extremely important role in non-segregated education of learners with disabilities (Gajdzica, 2011) because this kind of education usually requires collaboration between teachers (subject teacher with special educator), between teachers and specialists (school psychologist, therapist), between teachers and parents, and, of course, between teachers and learners. The essence of collaboration is to help one another in the achievement of goals, and an important feature of collaboration (in praxeological terms) is the coordination of sub-tasks envisaged by the division of labour (Pszczołowski, 1978). In the Polish realities of inclusive education, co-teaching is rare, and teachers also experience shortages in the field of specialist support (e. g., psychologists, therapists) (Nowak, 2020), which in practice limits day-to-day collaboration and probably explains the slightly lower rating of its significance.

The analysis performed with the selected factors shows, just like in the case of the previously analysed elements of inclusive education, that the teachers' rating of collaboration and leadership varies. Consequently, the teachers' point of view revealed in this respect requires acknowledging the importance of certain sociodemographic as well as job- and employment-related factors.

As a starting point, it should be emphasised that both collaboration and leadership were rated significantly higher by the teachers surveyed in 2020. The significantly less favourable rating expressed by the teachers surveyed in 2022 reveals the adverse changes taking place in their perception of inclusive education, already signalled earlier. The profound transformations are somewhat confirmed by the medium to high effect size found, captured especially within the area of leadership.

The higher rating of leadership compared to collaboration in inclusive education was found regardless of the period in which the teachers were surveyed. However, the degree of this rating can be interpreted in the context of other factors. Gender was found to be a variable differentiating the rating, but only among the teachers surveyed in 2020. Female teachers rated leadership in inclusive education significantly higher compared to male teachers. Age correlated positively (albeit weakly) with leadership rating, but only in the group of teachers surveyed in 2022. Higher ratings were expressed by older teachers. Urban teachers also rated leadership in inclusive education higher, with an emphasis on leaders being active in managing change and uncertainties, as well as in setting a vision and values conducive to inclusion of all learners.

We conclude on the basis of the analyses performed that the rating of leadership in inclusive education is higher in teachers with longer job seniority and longer length of service at their current place of employment. However, this relationship was recorded only among the teachers surveyed in 2022. The type of school where the teachers were employed, taken into account in the analyses, was found to be a non-significant factor in the teachers' rating of leadership in inclusive education. In contrast, significant variation within this rating was found with regard to another variable, namely the level taught. It is worth emphasising that the level taught differentiated this rating in a varied manner depending on the period in which the teachers were surveyed. In fact, leadership was rated highest by pre-school teachers in 2020, who emphasised this element of inclusive education much more strongly than teachers employed at other levels of education. In turn, among the teachers surveyed in 2022, the most favourable rating of leadership was identified in the case of those working at primary school with all levels. They expressed a significantly higher rating than the other teacher groups. It is worth highlighting at this point the differences noticeable between teachers employed at different stages of education with regard to their rating of the specific aspects of leadership. The results obtained here point to a difference in views on the leadership element in inclusive education among teachers. In particular, the clear variation among the teachers surveyed in 2022 and employed at the various educational levels may suggest the operation of certain unique factors, activated at that time with regard to the respective educational levels, and relevant for the teachers' rating of leadership.

The teachers' rating of collaboration in inclusive education was found to depend on various factors, which helps to outline a specific context for its interpretation. An analysis of the role of gender shows its significance for this rating, but only among the teachers surveyed in 2020. In contrast to male teachers, female teachers rated collaboration in inclusive education significantly higher. The second sociodemographic variable taken into account did not show any association with this rating. In turn, place of residence proved to be a differentiating variable, but only among the teachers surveyed in 2020. On the basis of the analyses, we conclude that urban teachers rate collaboration in inclusive education significantly higher, especially in areas such as working with parents to raise learners' aspirations and achievements, and designing support activities. They appreciated to a far greater extent the school's initiatives aimed at meeting with parents and discussing issues important to them together. On the basis of the analysis, we can also draw a conclusion concerning the relationship between the rating of collaboration in inclusive education and job seniority as well as length of service at the current place of employment. A higher rating is associated with longer job seniority of teachers, as well as with longer length of service at the current school. In turn, the type of school significantly differentiated this rating in teachers, but only among those surveyed in 2020. State school teachers expressed a higher rating, with a favourable attitude towards the school's networking with local entities and its collaboration with various entities capable of providing support to learners if needed. The last job-related variable taken into account, i.e. the level taught, also proved to be important for the rating of collaboration in inclusive education expressed by teachers. This variation was noticeable among teachers regardless of the period in which they were surveyed. However, the role of this variable in the ratings expressed by teachers surveyed in 2020 and 2022 was different. In the former group, the highest rating of collaboration was expressed by pre-school teachers. In contrast, teachers surveyed in 2022 and teaching all primary school levels formulated the highest rating in this respect.

Generally, effective collaboration between subject teachers and special educators in co-teaching is determined by a number of factors, including those related to the organisation and preparation of the collaboration, the methods of selecting teachers for collaboration, teachers' personality traits and dyadic communication styles, professional preparation for co-teaching as part of teacher and special educator training programmes, and the characteristics of learner teams (Szumski et al., 2021). As a result, as research shows, this often fails to produce the expected results (Jurkowski & Mueller, 2018), although there are also findings showing positive effects of collaboration, especially in terms of the benefits for teachers' professional development (Austin, 2001), or the reinforcement of positive attitudes towards inclusive education (Paulsrud & Nilholm, 2023).

The results mentioned here are consistent with those previously highlighted with regard to the rating of leadership in inclusive education. Consequently, the assessment of these two elements of inclusive education, namely collaboration and leadership, is extremely complex and requires various factors to be taken into account during interpretation, including in particular the level of education taught.

Chapter 8.
Impact of diverse learner needs on the curriculum – teachers' rating

Curriculum in inclusive education as rated by teachers – comparative analysis of 2020 and 2022 study results

In inclusive education, the curriculum is a key element in the pursuit of goals taking concrete shape in the realisation of the development potential of individual learners, as they acquire specific knowledge and skills. By definition, its design and implementation methods are based on taking into account the diverse individual needs and abilities of learners. However, to what extent the theoretical, ideological postulates for the implementation of the curriculum among learners with different cognitive, social/emotional and cultural competences are reflected in the practice of education is still an open question. The answers are sought above all in the point of view displayed by the teachers, those directly involved in the entire process of preparation and implementation of the curriculum in inclusive education. Consequently, the teachers' assessment of the curriculum addressed to learners with diverse needs and abilities was analysed. The analysis took into account two measurements, in 2020 and in 2022, sociodemographic variables: gender, age and place of residence, as well as job- and employment-related factors (seniority, length of service at the current school, type of school, and the level of education taught).

At the first stage of the analysis, we focused on collating the results in terms of the ratings concerning curriculum design in inclusive education, expressed by the teachers surveyed in 2020 and 2022. The results obtained point to statistically significant differences between these groups of teachers, but with a low effect size found both in the overall rating and with regard to the specific aspects related to curriculum design and implementation in inclusive education (Table 40). The teachers surveyed in 2020 scored significantly higher in their ratings of the design and implementation of the curriculum in inclusive education compared to the teachers surveyed in 2022.

Table 40. Curriculum in inclusive education as rated by the teachers surveyed in 2020 and 2022.

Teachers' rating	Teachers surveyed in 2020		Teachers surveyed in 2022		df	t-test	p	Cohen's d
	M	SD	M	SD				
Overall rating								
Curriculum	34.63	3.87	33.16	4.75	6,040	13.31	<0.001	0.206
Specific ratings								
The school implements curricula that take into account fundamental principles, such as appropriate scope and selection of content, coherence, relevance, and validity	4.61	0.51	4.48	0.59	6,040	9.24	<0.001	0.165
The school curricula provide learning opportunities for all learners	4.57	0.57	4.38	0.70	6,040	11.71	<0.001	0.116
The school curricula provide flexibility for teachers in the planning of realistic and challenging learning opportunities for all learners	4.36	0.62	4.15	0.77	6,040	11.54	<0.001	0.128
The school curricula make it possible for learners to choose/plan their individual learning curriculum	3.85	0.57	3.67	0.65	6,040	7.84	<0.001	0.109
The learners' well-being is a priority in the school curriculum	4.47	0.77	4.24	0.80	6,040	12.97	<0.001	0.240
The school curricula support effective transition between the individual stages of education	4.30	0.56	4.09	0.61	6,040	11.53	<0.001	0.336
Extra-curricular and social skill building activities are planned, engaging all learners	4.17	0.58	4.01	0.60	6,040	7.38	<0.001	0.180
The assessment framework adopted makes it possible to recognise wider achievements (e.g., social, sporting, artistic), as well as academic achievements	4.30	0.53	4.14	0.57	6,040	9.32	<0.001	0.137

M – arithmetic mean; SD – standard deviation; t – Student's t-test for independent data

Curriculum in inclusive education as rated by the teachers surveyed in 2020 – importance of sociodemographic as well as job- and employment-related variables

A further part of the analyses involved testing the importance of sociodemographic as well as job- and employment-related variables in the rating of the curriculum in inclusive education expressed by the teachers surveyed in 2020. In the course of the analyses performed, we found that the gender of teachers in this group significantly differentiated their rating of curriculum design and implementation in inclusive education. The results obtained are included in Table 41.

Female teachers rated the design and implementation of the curriculum in inclusive education significantly higher compared to male teachers. They had a much more positive opinion on the aspect of schools implementing the curricula on the basis of principles that obligate them to ensure appropriate content selection, coherence, relevance, and validity. Female teachers are significantly more convinced than male teachers that curricula in inclusive education take into account the learning opportunities of all learners, and provide teachers with flexibility in the planning of the learning process for learners with diverse needs and competences.

The teachers' age did not correlate statistically significantly with their rating of the curriculum in inclusive education ($r=-0.020$, $p=0.204$) either. A test of the place of residence variable also showed the lack of significant impact on the teachers' ratings ($M_{urban\ teachers}=34.70$, $SD=3.90$, $M_{rural\ teachers}=34.52$, $t=1.23$, $p=0.218$). Furthermore, similar results were obtained in the case of the type of school where the teachers were employed. The rating concerning the design of teaching in inclusive education expressed by teachers working at state schools was not statistically significantly different from that expressed by teachers working in non-state schools ($M_{state\ school\ teachers}=34.62$, $SD=3.87$, $M_{non-state\ school\ teachers}=34.72$, $SD=3.91$, Mann-Whitney $U=-0.41$, $p=0.681$). Job seniority and length of service at the current workplace are not statistically significantly associated with the teachers' rating ($r=0.014$, $p=0.422$; $r=0.012$, $p=0.431$, respectively). It is worth emphasising that the level of education taught by the teachers surveyed in 2020 did not statistically significantly differentiate their rating of the design of the curriculum in inclusive education either ($M_{pre-school\ teachers}=34.56$, $SD=4.16$; $M_{primary\ school\ levels\ 1\ to\ 3\ teachers}=34.68$, $SD=3.54$; $M_{primary\ school\ levels\ 4\ to\ 8\ teachers}=35.62$, $SD=3.20$; $M_{all\ primary\ school\ levels\ teachers}=34.71$, $SD=3.75$; $M_{secondary\ school\ teachers}=34.53$, $SD=3.88$; $F=0.49$; $p=0.742$).

Table 41. Impact of teachers' gender on the rating of curriculum by the teachers surveyed in 2020

Teachers' rating	Female teachers		Male teachers		df	U-test	p
	M	SD	M	SD			
Overall rating							
Curriculum	34.69	3.89	33.52	4.01	3,186	3.12	0.039
Specific ratings							
The school implements curricula that take into account fundamental principles, such as appropriate scope and selection of content, coherence, relevance, and validity	4.63	0.72	4.49	0.66	3,186	2.11	0.031
The school curricula provide learning opportunities for all learners	4.59	0.59	4.54	0.55	3,186	2.19	0.029
The school curricula provide flexibility for teachers in the planning of realistic and challenging learning opportunities for all learners	4.38	0.63	4.33	0.66	3,186	2.15	0.033
The school curricula make it possible for learners to choose/plan their individual learning curriculum	3.86	0.55	3.83	0.67	3,186	0.99	0.322
The learners' well-being is a priority in the school curriculum	4.48	0.63	4.34	0.70	3,186	1.91	0.051
The school curricula support effective transition between the individual stages of education	4.31	0.65	4.30	0.68	3,186	0.14	0.887
Extra-curricular and social skill building activities are planned, engaging all learners	4.16	0.77	4.18	0.75	3,186	-0.77	0.876
The assessment framework adopted makes it possible to recognise wider achievement (e.g., social, sporting, artistic), as well as academic achievements	4.30	0.67	4.25	0.69	3,186	0.98	0.112

M – arithmetic mean; SD – standard deviation; U – Mann-Whitney U-test

Curriculum in inclusive education as rated by the teachers surveyed in 2022 – importance of sociodemographic as well as job- and employment-related variables

The teachers surveyed in 2022 achieved slightly different results in their ratings of curriculum design in inclusive education in the context of the sociodemographic as well as job- and employment-related variables taken into account, compared to the teachers surveyed in 2020. In the case of the teachers' gender, similar results were obtained indicating the absence of any statistically significant difference between female and male teachers in the ratings expressed ($M_{female\ teachers}=33.17$, SD=4.74; $M_{male\ teachers}=33.04$, Mann-Whitney U=0.48, p=0.626). Just like in the group of teachers surveyed in 2020, the place of residence did not significantly differentiate the rating of the curriculum in inclusive education ($M_{urban\ teachers}=33.05$, SD=4.93, $M_{rural\ teachers}=33.32$, t=-1.49, p=0.137). Age, on the other hand, correlated significantly and positively with the teachers' ratings. Older teachers rated aspects of curriculum design in inclusive education lower (r=0.270, p<0.001). Teachers from state and non-state schools expressed significantly different ratings with regard to the aspect analysed here (Table 42).

Table 42. Impact of the school type (state/non-state) on the rating of the curriculum in inclusive education by the teachers surveyed in 2022

Teachers' rating	State school teachers		Non-state school teachers		df	U-test	p
	M	SD	M	SD			
Overall rating							
Curriculum	32.18	4.71	33.98	4.76	2,851	-3.51	0.011
Specific ratings							
The school implements curricula that take into account fundamental principles, such as appropriate scope and selection of content, coherence, relevance, and validity	4.41	0.66	4.51	0.70	2,851	-1.65	0.056
The school curricula provide learning opportunities for all learners	4.38	0.77	4.34	0.71	2,851	0.66	0.521
The school curricula provide flexibility for teachers in the planning of realistic and challenging learning opportunities for all learners	4.15	0.67	4.19	0.62	2,851	-0.45	0.712
The school curricula make it possible for learners to choose/plan their individual learning curriculum	3.52	0.64	3.77	0.59	2,851	-4.15	0.003
The learners' well-being is a priority in the school curriculum	3.16	0.55	3.29	0.62	2,851	-5.02	0.017
The school curricula support effective transition between the individual stages of education	3.97	0.59	4.18	0.64	2,851	-0.89	0.113
Extra-curricular and social skill building activities are planned, engaging all learners	4.10	0.66	4.25	0.72	2,851	-3.78	0.024
The assessment framework adopted makes it possible to recognise wider achievement (e.g., social, sporting, artistic), as well as academic achievements	4.13	0.67	4.14	0.71	2,851	-0.28	0.892

M – arithmetic mean; SD – standard deviation; U – Mann-Whitney U-test

On the basis of the analysis, we conclude that the teachers surveyed in 2022 working in non-state schools rated the design and implementation of the curriculum in inclusive education significantly higher compared to teachers working at state schools. Significant differences between these two groups of teachers were found with regard to the ratings concerning specific issues related to the design or implementation of the curriculum. Non-state school teachers expressed a far more positive opinion on the item stating that the curricula implemented in inclusive education provide learners with the opportunity to plan their individual learning process. They also pay attention to a significantly greater extent to the fact that the curriculum designed prioritises the well-being of each learner, with their individual needs and capabilities. Furthermore, they emphasise much more strongly that extra-curricular and social skill building activities are planned for all learners included in the education process.

On the basis of the correlation analysis, we found job seniority to be significantly and positively associated with the teachers' ratings of curriculum design in inclusive education. Teachers with longer job seniority rated the process of curriculum design and implementation higher. The correlation found points to a weak strength of association between these variables ($r=0.140$, $p<0.021$). In addition, teachers with longer length of service at their current school rated the aspect analysed here higher. However, also in this case, the correlation found is weak ($r=0.180$, $p<0.001$). Teachers employed at different levels expressed significantly different ratings concerning curriculum design in inclusive education. The results obtained in this respect are presented in Table 43.

Table 43. Impact of the level taught on the rating of curriculum in inclusive education by the teachers surveyed in 2022

Rating	Pre-school teachers (1)		Teachers of primary school levels 1 to 3 (2)		Teachers of primary school levels 4 to 8 (3)		Teachers of all primary school levels (4)		Secondary school teachers (5)		One-way ANOVA		
	M	SD	M	SD	M	SD	M	SD	M	SD	F	Inter-group comparison	p
Curriculum							Overall rating						
Curriculum	32.80	4.94	33.20	4.62	33.03	4.73	33.58	4.47	32.89	5.09	2.84*	1–4 3–4 4–5	0.005 0.039 0.008
							Specific ratings						
1	4.46	0.58	4.47	0.61	4.48	0.65	4.50	0.70	4.49	0.55	0.54	-	
2	4.34	0.66	4.38	0.72	4.34	0.71	4.41	0.64	4.38	0.63	1.23	-	
3	4.16	0.74	4.15	0.75	4.09	0.69	4.19	0.66	4.16	0.64	1.35	-	
4	3.65	0.62	3.70	0.65	3.65	0.70	3.69	0.67	3.64	0.63	0.44	-	
5	4.27	0.77	4.21	0.80	4.23	0.65	4.30	0.71	4.15	0.69	3.60**	1–5 2–4 4–5	0.010 0.040 <0.001
6	4.09	0.81	4.10	0.76	4.11	0.72	4.13	0.76	4.04	0.81	1.25	-	
7	3.84	0.72	4.05	0.76	4.02	0.74	4.14	0.69	3.93	0.73	10.02***	1–2 1–3 1–4 2–5 3–4 4–5	<0.001 0.001 <0.001 0.030 0.021 <0.001

Table 43 (Continued)

Rating	Pre-school teachers (1)		Teachers of primary school levels 1 to 3 (2)		Teachers of primary school levels 4 to 8 (3)		Teachers of all primary school levels (4)		Secondary school teachers (5)		One-way ANOVA		
	M	SD	M	SD	M	SD	M	SD	M	SD	F	Inter-group comparison	p
8	3.98	0.80	4.16	0.76	4.14	0.69	4.23	0.70	4.11	0.75	8.71***	1–2	<0.001
												1–3	0.001
												1–4	<0.001
												1–5	0.005
												3–4	0.028
												4–5	0.004

1: The school implements curricula that take into account fundamental principles, such as appropriate scope and selection of content, coherence, relevance, and validity; 2: The school curricula provide learning opportunities for all learners; 3: The school curricula provide flexibility for teachers in the planning of realistic and challenging learning opportunities for all learners; 4: The school curricula make it possible for learners to choose/ plan their individual learning curriculum; 5: The learners' well-being is a priority in the school curriculum; 6: The school curricula support effective transition between the individual stages of education; 7: Extra-curricular and social skill building activities are planned, engaging all learners; 8: The assessment framework adopted makes it possible to recognise wider achievement (e.g., social, sporting, artistic), as well as academic achievements

Conclusion and discussion

On the basis of the analysis, we conclude that teachers of all primary school levels scored highest in the rating of curriculum design and implementation in inclusive education. They differ statistically significantly in this respect from preschool teachers and secondary school teachers. These findings fit within the broader trends of stronger acceptance of the curriculum in inclusive education by teachers working at higher levels of education (Moltó, 2003). Naturally, this study did not demonstrate how teachers interpreted the formula for adapting the curriculum to the capabilities of all learners. It is worth bearing in mind that the relatively high level of approval indicated does not necessarily imply only positive consequences in practice. Research shows that adaptation of the general curriculum to the needs and capabilities of learners with disabilities (especially intellectual disabilities) is sometimes embedded in the concept of compensatory education aimed at correcting deficiencies outside mainstream education, e.g. as part of remedial classes (Otukile-Mongwaketseet al., 2016).

The variation between the different groups of teachers in the rating area analysed here was noticeable in certain specific aspects. Firstly, teachers of all primary school levels emphasise much more the fact that the learner's well-being is a priority in the design and implementation of the curriculum. They differ statistically significantly in this respect from primary school levels 1 to 3 teachers and secondary school teachers. The latter group scored significantly lower on this rating compared to pre-school teachers. Secondly, also teachers of all primary school levels are most strongly convinced that the curriculum implemented in inclusive education takes into account extra-curricular and social skill building activities for all learners. In this respect, they scored significantly higher than preschool teachers, primary school levels 4 to 8 teachers, and secondary school teachers. It is worth emphasising that with regard to this aspect of curriculum rating, pre-school teachers scored lowest, significantly lower than primary school levels 1 to 3 teachers, primary school levels 4 to 8 teachers and all primary school levels teachers. A similar rating was also recorded in relation to the item stating that the assessment framework adopted in relation to curriculum implementation ensures that a wide range of learners' achievements (academic, social, sporting or artistic) are recognised. Pre-school teachers scored lowest here, significantly lower compared to all the other teacher groups. In turn, teachers of all primary school levels expressed the highest rating with regard to this aspect, making them statistically significantly different from primary school teachers, but only those teaching levels 4 to 8, and secondary school teachers.

Summing up the teachers' ratings concerning the design and implementation of the curriculum in inclusive education, we can point to certain factors that may be relevant to its interpretation. Consistently with the rating of all the previous elements of inclusive education, the teachers surveyed in 2022 rated the curriculum much lower. This is another context worth taking into account when discussing teachers' perceptions of inclusive education at a time of particular, surprising transformations and changing external circumstances. It is worth noting that, compared to the other previously analysed elements of inclusive education, the rating of the curriculum was least subject to variation depending on the sociodemographic as well as job- and employment-related variables taken into account. We can assume that teachers rate curriculum design and implementation, which in a sense is formally regulated, quite unambiguously, with a small role played by certain contextual factors. Gender was found, for instance, to differentiate this rating, but only among the teachers surveyed in 2020. Female teachers expressed a much higher rating, emphasising above all the compatibility of the school's curriculum with the capabilities of all learners. Age correlated positively with the rating of curriculum design, but only among the teachers surveyed in 2022. Older teachers expressed a higher rating. The teachers' place of residence was not a differentiating factor in their rating of curriculum design and implementation in inclusive education. The type of school the teachers were employed at was relevant only for the ratings expressed by the teachers surveyed in 2022. Ratings by teachers from non-state schools were higher, as they pointed for example to the individualisation of curricula, to the well-being of every learner being taken into account in their design, etc. Also in this group of teachers, i.e. those surveyed in 2022, job seniority and length of service at the current place of employment were associated with the rating of curriculum development and implementation in inclusive education. A higher rating given by teachers was associated with longer job seniority, including longer length of service at the current school. The last job- and employment-related variable analysed, i.e. the level taught, differentiated this rating, but only among the teachers surveyed in 2022. Teachers working at primary schools teaching all levels rated the design and implementation of the curriculum in inclusive education significantly higher compared to the other teacher groups. It is therefore worth emphasising that the job- and employment-related variables adopted were significant for this rating only among the teachers surveyed in 2022. On this basis, we can predict that the transformations taking place during this period had a significant impact on the pursuit of the teaching profession in inclusive education. Hence, occupation-related factors that define functioning within the profession may have played a particular role in the rating of the implementation of the curriculum in inclusive education.

Research limitations

The research provided a number of interesting and significant findings with regard to the views on inclusive education and teaching of learners with diverse educational needs. However, the results obtained are not free from certain limitations, the most important being the following:

1) The research covered a wide range of professional experiences of teachers working at different levels of mainstream education, from pre-school to secondary schools. However, the studies only considered selected socio-demographic and job-related variables. Although we consider them particularly relevant in analyses of opinions on the functioning of inclusive education in Poland, they nevertheless provide merely a preliminary diagnosis in this respect. In future research, it would be important to test other factors, such as those related to teachers' self-assessment of working with learners with diverse learning needs, as well as the environmental and cultural determinants of effective education for all learners.

2) In the research, we used a self-reporting tool for describing the work of the mainstream school in the context of the indicators of implementation of education for all learners, based on the subjective opinion of the respondents. Supplementing the research results with objective data from school documentation would make it possible to obtain a complete picture of the implementation of this form of education in Polish schools, at the various educational levels.

3) The research conducted revealed a number of significant differences in the opinions of the teachers surveyed, working at different levels of education. The results show, in fact, that education for all, although relatively clear in terms of the underlying assumptions, may demonstrate significant variation in terms of the details of organisation and implementation depending on the stage of education, and thus on the developmental age of the learners. It is therefore important to take a closer look at inclusive education implemented at the pre-school, primary, and secondary school levels. Identifying its spe-

cificities and determinants would provide a basis to design specific methodological, organisational, or legislative solutions.

4) The longitudinal study design used revealed statistically significant differences between the results obtained in 2020 and in 2022. Thus, we can identify the change that took place in teachers' opinions on the organisation and implementation of education for all as a certain reaction to the transformations taking place over that time: the introduction of new system solutions and the admission of Ukrainian refugees to Polish schools. The studies conducted at those particular moments reflected the reality prevailing at the given time: most likely that of a relative disruption in mainstream education and of some experimentation rather than conscious and reflective education oriented towards cultivating difference. They provide a certain diagnosis of a particular period of implementation of inclusive education in a Polish school, outlining the unique social and cultural context. On the other hand, they do not make it possible to understand how the process of mainstreaming of all learners in pre-school and school facilities actually took place and what the effects of that process were. It would be important in this respect to continue the research in a third time frame, in the context of the further changes currently being designed related to inclusive education. In doing so, it would be important to capture the perceived consequences of the contexts taken into account in the 2020 and 2022 studies (refugeeism and systemic changes in Polish education).

5) The research designed covered merely a certain group of teachers. In order to obtain a complete picture of the implementation of education for learners with diverse learning needs, it would be useful to analyse the opinions of other people involved in the education process, including headmasters/headmistresses, school educators, parents, and the learners themselves.

Conclusion

We examined the research results presented and discussed here in a cross-sectional and longitudinal perspective.

The former shows the data considered in the aspect of different variables separately in 2020 and 2022. Averaging the data from both measurements, we should describe the degree of approval among Polish teachers of the basic assumptions underlying inclusive education as high. This result may be surprising in the context of many other studies showing neutral or negative attitudes towards the inclusion of learners with special educational needs in mainstream schools. For example, De Boer, Pijl, and Minnaert (2011), in an extensive meta-analysis involving a review of 26 studies published between 1998 and 2008, did not find a single study showing clearly positive results. In another large meta-analysis of studies of attitudes towards inclusive education covering the period between 2000 and 2020, including as many as 212 studies in 55 countries, the authors noted moderately positive attitudes, corresponding to the first positive point of the scale ("somewhat agree") (Guillemot et al., 2020). Against this background, the results obtained in our study should be described as optimistic. This optimism, however, loses its lustre in the perspective of a longitudinal analysis.

The second perspective shows a comparison of data from two measurements performed in 2020 and 2022. The relatively short two-year time frame should apparently not significantly differentiate the results of the study. However, a detailed analysis of the data revealed statistically significant differences in virtually all the areas examined: teachers' beliefs about the legitimacy of education for all, perception of learners' subjectivity in inclusive education, acceptance of the assumptions of supportive education / in inclusive education, perception of leadership and collaboration, and the aspect of curriculum faced with learner diversity. As shown by the data analysis, the high rate of acceptance of the basic assumptions underlying inclusive education in the first measurement decreased significantly. When looking for the determinants of the state of affairs diagnosed, two events should be noted. The first one involves the significant increase in the number of learners from Ukraine, which proved to pose a significant educational challenge for the whole Polish educational system. The impact of this change was felt especially by teachers previously unprepared for the challenges related to working with a culturally diverse group. As shown by some of the first broader studies diagnosing the feelings and needs of Polish teachers, the presence of learners from Ukrainian refugee families represented a significant additional burden in the daily work of education and teaching (Pyżalski et al., 2022). The second event was the publication of two drafts for reforming the Polish educational system by the then Ministry of National Education (currently the Ministry of Education and Science): *Model edukacji dla wszystkich* [*A Model of Education for All*] (2020) and *Wspieranie podnoszenia jakości edukacji włączającej w Polsce* [*Supporting the Improvement of Quality of Inclusive Education in Poland*] (2020). The documents contained a wide range of changes aimed at strengthening inclusive education, which caused a lot of controversy reinforced by political disputes and a tradition of looking critically at the not entirely well-prepared earlier reforms of the education system in Poland (Świątkiewicz-Mośny,2014). In addition, teachers' negative feelings may also have been reinforced by the prolonged remote teaching (although the first measurement was performed during the initial pandemic period) and the deteriorating economic situation affecting the society at large.

A significant aim of the research also involved identifying sociodemographic variables (gender, age and place of residence), as well as variables related to the occupation and employment of the teachers surveyed (job seniority, length of service at the current school, type of school and level of education taught). The associations between the indicated variables and the teachers' declarations examined in the 2020 and 2022 cross-sectional surveys.

A detailed analysis of the data showed a differentiated relationship of sociodemographic variables and variables related to the teachers' job seniority and employment with their declarations. An example collation within the area of the declarations concerning the validity of inclusive education is presented in Table 44.

Table 44. Relationship of sociodemographic variables and variables related to teachers' job seniority and employment with declarations on the validity of inclusive education

Independent variables	Generalised statements on the validity of inclusive education differentiated by (+), not differentiated by (-)	
	2020 survey	2022 survey
Gender	+ (stronger approval of female teachers)	-

Table 44 *(Continued)*

	Generalised statements on the validity of inclusive education differentiated by (+), not differentiated by (-)	
Independent variables	**2020 survey**	**2022 survey**
Age	+ (stronger approval of younger teachers)	-
Place of residence	+ (stronger approval of urban teachers)	-
Job seniority	-	+ (stronger approval of teachers with longer seniority)
Type of school/ pre-school	+ (stronger approval of teachers employed at non-state facilities)	-
Level taught	+ (stronger approval of teachers employed at lower education levels)	+ (stronger approval of teachers employed at lower education levels)

In general, the independent variables studied differentiated the declarations far more frequently in the first survey, which may be an effect of the flattening of the declarations in 2022. Job seniority was found to be the only variable differentiating the declarations in the second measurement.

In turn, the level of education taught was found to differentiate the declarations on the validity of inclusive education in both measurements, which is also confirmed by other studies (Gigante & Gilmore,2020). A similar trend was also revealed in the other areas of the research.

The results of the studies can be considered from several theoretical perspectives. The first one refers to the development stage of inclusive education. Let us point out that, according to an analysis of the definition of the form of education discussed, it is possible to distinguish four stages thereof: from perceiving inclusive education mainly as the physical presence of learners with diverse learning and socialisation difficulties in the mainstream classroom, to focusing primarily on the special educational needs of the learners being included, to treating inclusive education as a form of quality education for all learners and perceiving the mainstream school as a community constituted on an inclusive culture (Göransson & Nilholm, 2014). The set of items for acceptance used in the study place inclusive education in the third and fourth perspectives. This is exemplified for instance by the following items: teachers are responsible for the learning/teaching of all learners in the classroom; teachers take steps to address the differentiated/differentiated needs of all learners in the classroom, teachers personalise the learning process for all learners *(Kwestionariusz samooceny pracy szkoły, wersja polska [Raising Achievement Self-Review, Polish version]*, 2020). These items correspond to the definitions of inclusive education emphasising that school is a place of education for all children, where the needs of every learner are met (Thomazet, 2009). Such statements are also found in the definitions present in the Polish literature *(Model edukacji dla wszystkich* 2020; Jachimczak & Podgórska-Jachnik, 2023). The research results indicate, therefore, that the teachers surveyed in the first measurement were closer to the concept of inclusive education placed in the perspective of perceiving it as quality education for all learners. In contrast, the second measurement showed a decline in this area. We can assume that the weaker acceptance of the assumptions indicated signifies a shift towards perceiving inclusive education as education aimed at meeting the needs of selected learners and strengthening the role of specialist support. It is worth adding that these aspects are also rooted in other research and opinions showing the difficulties related to inclusion implemented with selected groups of learners, including those with more profound disabilities (especially intellectual disabilities) (Avramidis et al., 2000; Avramidis & Norwich, 2002; Hashmi et al., 2017).

The second perspective relates to the issue of reforming the educational system, and in fact to the education reform in course. As schools undergo constant transformation, inclusive education can play the role of a certain catalyst for change (Hodkinson, 2007; Savolainenet al., 2012; Hajisoteriou & Sorkos, 2022). Arguably, this change involves the desire to extend quality teaching to cover all learners in the classroom. Changing schools for the better requires vision, skills, incentives, resources, and an action plan (Robinson & Aronica, 2016). The research presented here fits into the first of the elements indicated, i. e. vision. The degree of teachers' acceptance of specific statements building concrete assumptions underlying quality education for all learners is an indicator of acceptance of the school's vision for change. Its implementation requires adequate resources, among other things. Their absence leads to frustration (ibid.) The results of the research presented here indicate that this vision is perceived positively by the majority of Polish teachers. In turn, the reduced rate of acceptance recorded in the second measurement may have been caused by the frustration felt in relation to the insufficient resources required for its implementation, for instance as a result of the appearance of large numbers of Ukrainian learners in the Polish educational system.

The third perspective presents the issues discussed here in the context of school culture and social change. Inclusive school culture is a particular microclimate. It is a derivative of the broad school culture (a shared system of norms and values as well as behavioural patterns and rituals of teachers, learners, management, and non-teaching staff) and the culture surrounding the school (determined by political, religious, economic, and other factors). The school microclimate remains in feedback with the surrounding local environment/social climate (Zamkowska, 2017; Jachimczak, 2021). On the one hand, the school reproduces the social climate and, on the other hand, it co-creates it by educating the learners who, once they finish school, carry its climate into the social environment. One element of the school microclimate includes the attitudes of teachers towards inclusive education. Similarly to the whole climate, they are an intertwining of local and global culture with the values and norms produced and recognised at school.

The change of teachers' attitudes fit within social change understood as the difference between the state of a social system (group, organisation) at a certain point in time and the state of the same system at another point in time (Sztompka, 2012). These states may differ in terms of the following:

- system composition (e.g., the arrival of large numbers of refugees or immigrants), with new social movements emerging, resulting in social reforms;
- system structure change (e.g., the emergence of new interactional, interest, normative structures), as a result of which people begin to adhere to new values, follow new norms, play new social roles;
- changes in the functions performed by elements of the general public (e.g., change in the traditional functions of family, school);
- system boundary changes (e.g., merger or division of traditionally operating institutions);
- changes in the system environment (e.g., urbanisation changes) (Sztompka, 2012).

The decreased acceptance of inclusive education recorded in the second measurement is a consequence of the social changes in Poland indicated above. For about a dozen years now, the composition of the social system has been changing due to an ageing population and the emergence of an increasingly numerous group of economic migrants and, after 2020, also of war refugees. As a result, a change also arises in the composition of the school system (an increase in the mean age of teachers and in the presence of children from immigrant and refugee families). In this context, it is worth noting that teachers' job seniority proved to be one of the two variables (apart from the level taught) differentiating their views on the validity of inclusive education. The change in the system structure can be seen in the emergence of new groups of interest. Example of this are organisations that bring together people who deny the legitimacy of inclusive education (e.g., *Ruch Ochrony Szkoły*, 2022). In turn, the change of the school's function can be seen, among other things, in the extent of psychological and pedagogical support being reinforced as a result of the emergence of an increasing number of learners with special development needs. This leads to the school's staff being expanded to include permanently employed therapists, special educators, and psychologists, and to its tasks being supplemented by therapeutic ones.

The result of this is a change in the attitudes of teachers who, in many respects, are somewhat more sceptical of the assumptions underlying quality education for all learners, which perhaps justifies the findings of the research presented here.

Nevertheless, the results obtained should be considered optimistic. They show the positive attitude of Polish teachers of mainstream schools and pre-schools towards the assumptions underlying inclusive education. The study also made it possible to identify areas of greater concern, which is an indicator for seeking new or reinforcing existing organisational solutions aimed at strengthening quality education for all learners.

The research presented here also made it possible to capture the change in teachers' declarations over a period that was short, but quite unique for the Polish educational system. We are convinced that the longitudinal studies initiated are worth continuing in the future, probably with the expansion of the interpretative contexts to include new categories of social events, which are difficult to predict at this point.

References

Ainscow. M., Miles. S. (2008). Making Education for All inclusive: where next?. *Prospects,* 38, 15–34.

Allan. J. (2007). *Rethinking Inclusive Education: The Philosophers of Difference in Practice* (Vol. 5). Springer Science & Business Media.

Austin. V.L. (2001). Teachers' beliefs about co-teaching. *Remedial and Special Education,* 22, 245–255.

Avramidis. E., & Norwich. B. (2002). *Teachers' attitudes towards integration/inclusion: a review of the literature. European Journal of Special Needs Education,* 17(2), 129–147.

Avramidis. E., Bayliss. P., & Burden, R. (2000). Student teachers' attitudes towards the inclusion of children with special educational needs in the ordinary school. *Teaching and Teacher Education,* 16(3), 277–293.

Aydin. H & Kaya. Y. (2019) Education for Syrian Refugees: The New Global Issue Facing Teachers and Principals in Turkey. *Educational Studies,* 55, 46–71.

Babbie. E. (2005). The Basics of Social Research. 3rd. Ed. Belmont, CA: Thomson/Wadsworth.

Babińska. M., Bilewicz. M., Górska. P., Toruńczyk-Ruiz. S., Wypych. M. (2022). Polacy wobec Ukraińców: Wyniki badań sondażowych zrealizowanych po inwazji rosyjskiej na Ukrainę w 2022 roku [Poles' Attitudes Towards Ukrainians: Results of Survey Research Following the Russian Invasion Against Ukraine in 2022]. *Nauka* [Science] 4, 37–58.

Bąbka. J., Podgruszewska. M. (2016). Polityka oświatowa wobec uczniów ze specjalnymi potrzebami edukacyjnymi w perspektywie lokalnej – na podstawie opinii nauczycieli małego miasta [Educational Policy Towards Learners with Special Needs in the Local Perspective – on the Basis of Opinions of Small-Town Teachers]. *Niepełnosprawność. Dyskursy Pedagogiki Specjalnej* [*Disability. Discourses of Special Pedagogy*], 22, 92–106.

Bałachowicz. J. (2017). Edukacja wczesnoszkolna w procesie zmiany. Dyskurs standardów czy dyskurs wartości? [Primary School Levels 1 to 3 Education in a Process of Change. Discourse of Standards or Discourse of Values?], *Lubelski Rocznik Pedagogiczny* [*Lublin Pedagogical Yearbook*], 36 (1), 11–27.

Barańska. M., Sirak. K. (2015). Poglądy osób związanych z oświatą na wspólne nauczanie dzieci o zróżnicowanych potrzebach edukacyjnych [Views of Individuals Associated with Education on Co-Teaching Children with Diverse Educational Needs], *Niepełnosprawność. Dyskursy Pedagogiki Specjalnej* [*Disability. Discourses of Special Pedagogy*], 20, 128–142.

Barnartt. S., Scotch. R. (2002). *Disability Protest. Contentious Politics 1970–1999,* Washington: Gallaudet University Press.

Barnová. S., Kožuchová. M., Krásna. S., Osaďan. R. (2022). Teachers' Professional Attitudes towards Inclusive Education. *Emerging Science Journal* 6, 13–24.

Bartnikowska. U., Wójcik. M. (2004). Zaniedbania w aspekcie triady: szkoła – rodzice – dziecko w kształceniu integracyjnym [Omissions in the Aspect of the School – Parents – Child Triad in Inclusive Education] (287–299). In: Z. Gajdzica, A. Klinik (eds.), *Wątki zaniedbane, zaniechane, nieobecne w procesie edukacji i wsparcia społecznego osób niepełnosprawnych [Neglected, Abandoned, Absent Themes in the Process of Education and Social Support of Disabled Persons]*. Katowice: Wydawnictwo Uniwersytetu Śląskiego.

Bartoňová. M. (2014). *Inkluzivní didaktika v základní škole se zřetelem na edukaci žáku s lehkým mentálním postižením*. Brno: Masarykova univerzita.

Bera. R., Korczyński. M. (2012). *Dystans społeczny emigrantów polskich wobec "Obcych" i "Innych" [Social Distance of Polish Emigrants Towards "Strangers" and "Others"]* UMCS: Lublin.

Boroń. A., Gromkowska-Melosik. A. (2022). *Ukraińskie uchodźczynie wojenne. Tożsamość, trauma, nadzieja [Ukrainian Female War Refugees. Identity, Trauma, Hope]*. Impuls: Kraków.

Byra. S., Domagała-Zyśk E. (2021). Multidimensional assessment of student teachers' self-esteem and attitudes towards inclusive education and people with disabilities. *Teaching Education* 33(3), 237–253.

Byra. S., Kazanowski Z. (2015). Postrzeganie kompetencji zawodowych nauczyciela w edukacji inkluzyjnej – próba pomiaru [Perception of Teachers' Professional Competencies in Inclusive Education – Measurement Attempt] (247–260). In: B. Szczupał. A. Giryński. G. Szumski (eds.) *W poszukiwaniu indywidualnych dróg wspierających wszechstronny rozwój osób z niepełnosprawnością [In Search of Individual Paths Supporting the Comprehensive Development of Persons with Disabilities]*. Warszawa. Wydawnictwo Akademii Pedagogiki Specjalnej.

Cekiera. R. (2022). *Uchodźcy, migranci i Kościół katolicki. Polska debata migracyjna po 215 roku w kontekście nauczania Kościoła katolickiego [Refugees, Migrants and the Catholic Church. The Post-2015 Polish Migration Debate in the Context of the Teachings of the Catholic Church]*. Warszawa: Biblioteka Więzi.

Chrzanowska, I. (2019). *Nauczyciele o szansach i barierach edukacji włączającej [Teachers on the Opportunities and Barriers of Inclusive Education]*. Warszawa: Wydawnictwo Naukowe PWN.

Chrzanowska, I. (2019a). Postawy wobec edukacji włączającej – jakie skutki [Attitudes Towards Inclusive Education – Effects]. In: I. Chrzanowska, G. Szumski (eds.), *Edukacja włączająca w przedszkolu i szkole [Inclusive Education in Pre-Schools and Schools]* (44–53). Warszawa: FRSE.

Ćwirynkało K., Żyta A. (2015). Przekonania nauczycieli na temat edukacji włączającej uczniów ze specjalnymi potrzebami edukacyjnymi [Teachers' Beliefs on Inclusive Education of Learners with Special Educational Needs]. *Szkoła Specjalna [Special Needs School]*, 4, 245–259.

Cytowska. B. (2016), Przegląd badań empirycznych nad inkluzją w edukacji [Review of Empirical Research on Inclusion in Education]. *Problemy Edukacji, Rehabilitacji,*

Socjalizacji Osób Niepełnosprawnych [*Problems of Education, Rehabilitation, Socialisation of Disabled Persons*], 22, 189–213.

Czerepaniak-Walczak. M. (2015), Kultura szkoły – o jej złożoności i wielowymiarowości [School Culture – Its Complex and Multifaceted Nature]. *Pedagogika Społeczna* [*Social Pedagogy*] 3 (57), 77–87.

De Boer. A., Pijl. S. J., & Minnaert. A. (2011). Regular primary schoolteachers' attitudes towards inclusive education: A review of the literature. *International Journal of Inclusive Education,* 15(3), 331–353.

Desombre. C., Delaval. M., Jury. M. (2021) Influence of Social Support on Teachers' *Attitudes Toward Inclusive Education. Front. Psychol.* 12, 1–7.

Dubas. E. (2017). O podmiotowości w kontekście pedagogicznym [On Subjectivity in the Pedagogical Context]. Edukacja Dorosłych [Adult Education], 2, 21–36.

Duszczyk. M., Kaczmarczyk. P. (2022). *War and migration: the recent influx from Ukraine into Poland and possible scenarios for the future. CMR Spotlight,* 4 (39). Downloaded from: https://www.migracje.uw.edu.pl/wp-content/uploads/2022/04/Spotlight-APRIL-2022.pdf (March 2023).

Dyjas-Pokorska. A. (2005). Badania trackingowe i panelowe [Tracking and Panel Studies]. In: P. B. Sztabiński, Z. Sawiński, F. Sztabiński (eds.): *Fieldwork jest sztuką. Jak dobrać respondenta, skłonić do udziału w wywiadzie, rzetelnie i sprawnie zrealizować badanie* [*Fieldwork Is an Art. How to Select the Respondent, Encourage Them to Participate in the Interview, and Conduct a Survey in a Reliable and Efficient Manner*] (237–252). Warszawa: Wydawnictwo IFiS PAD.

Dyson. A., & Forlin. C. (1999). An international perspective on inclusion. In: P. Engelbrecht. L. Green. S. Naicker. & L. Engelbrecht. (Eds.), *Inclusive Education in Action in South Africa* (22–44). Pretoria, South Africa: van Schaik.

Dyson. A., & Millward. A. (2000). *Schools and special needs: Issues of innovation and inclusion.* London: Paul Chapman.

Farrell. M. (1998). The role of the special educational needs co-ordinator: looking forward. *Support for Learning,* 13 (2), 82–86.

Friend. M., Cook. L. Hurley-Chamberlain. A., Shamberger. C. (2010). Co-Teaching: An Illustration of the Complexity of Collaboration in Special Education. *Journal of Educational and Psychological Consultation,* 20, 9–27.

Gajdzica, Z. (2011a). Opinie nauczycieli szkół ogólnodostępnych na temat edukacji włączającej uczniów z lekkim upośledzeniem umysłowym w kontekście toczącej się reformy kształcenia specjalnego [Opinions of Mainstream School Teachers on Inclusive Education of Learners with Mild Mental Disabilities in the Context of the Special Needs Education Reform in Progress] (56–79). In: Z. Gajdzica (ed.), *Uczeń z niepełnosprawnością w szkole ogólnodostępnej* [*Learners with Disabilities in Mainstream Schools*]. Sosnowiec: WSH.

Gajdzica. Z. (2011). *Sytuacje trudne w opinii nauczycieli klas integracyjnych* [*Situations Difficult in the Opinion of Inclusive Class Teachers*]. Kraków: Impuls.

Gajdzica. Z. (2013). *Uczniowie i studenci z obszaru pogranicza wobec sytuacji osób niepełnosprawnych w środowisku lokalnym – nastawienia i opinie* [*Learners and Students from the Borderland Area and the Situation of Disabled Persons in the Local Community – Attitudes and Opinions*]. Cieszyn – Skoczów: Stowarzyszenie Wsparcia Społecznego "Feniks".

Gajdzica. Z. (2019). Działanie i godność ludzka, jako kategorie konstytuujące dwie koncepcje inkluzji edukacyjnej uczniów z niepełnosprawnością [Human Dignity and Action as Categories Constituting Two Concepts of Educational Inclusion of Learners with Disabilities]. In: L. Pawelski, M. Rembierz (eds.) *Wychowywać (w sobie) mistrza [Raising a Master (Within Oneself)]* (177–188). Szczecinek: Polskie Stowarzyszenie Nauczycieli Twórczych.

Gajdzica. Z. (2020). *Uczeń z lekką niepełnosprawnością intelektualną w szkole ogólnodostępnej. Nauczyciele o (nie)zmienianej sytuacji w kontekście kultury szkoły inkluzyjnej [Learners with Mild Intellectual Disabilities in Mainstream Schools. Teachers on the (Un)Changing Situation in the Context of Inclusive Schooling.* Warszawa: Wydawnictwo Naukowe PWN.

Gajdzica. Z. (2022). Nieobecne lub zaniedbane w polskiej szkole formy wspierania nauczycieli w edukacji włączającej [Forms of Supporting Teachers in Inclusive Education Absent or Neglected in Polish Schools]. *Studia z Teorii Wychowania [Studies on the Theory of Education]*, 3(40), 13–27.

Gajdzica. Z., McWilliam. R., Potměšil. M, Ling. G. (2020). Inclusive Education of Learners with Disability – the Theory versus Reality. Peter Lang: Berlin, Bern, Bruxelles, New York, Oxford, Warszawa, Wien.

Gajdzica. Z., Skotnicka. B., Pawlik. S., Bełza-Gajdzica. M., Trojanowska. M., Prysak. D., Mrózek. S. (2021). *Analiza praktyki szkolnej i charakterystyka szkoły efektywnie realizującej edukację włączającą w praktyce – raport z badań [Analysis of School Practice and Description of a School Effectively Implementing Inclusive Education in Practice – Study Report].* Warszawa: MEiN. Downloaded from: https://www.ore.edu.pl/2021/11/a naliza-praktyki-szkolnej-i-charakterystyka-szkoly-efektywnie-realizujacej-edukacje-w laczajaca-w-praktyce-raport-z-badan/ (May 2021).

Gigante. J., & Gilmore. L. (2020). Australian preservice teachers' attitudes and perceived efficacy for teaching in inclusive classrooms. International Journal of Inclusive Education, 24(14), 1568–1577.

Gołdyka. L. (2013). *Pogranicze polsko-niemieckie jako przestrzeń socjalizacji [The German-Polish Borderland as a Space for Socialisation].* Warszawa: Scholar.

Göransson. K., Nilholm. C. (2014). Conceptual diversities and empirical shortcomings – a critical analysis of research on inclusive education. European Journal of Special Needs Education, 29 (3), 265–280.

Gordon-Gould. P., Hornby. G. (2023). *Inclusive education at the Crossroads. Exploring Effective Special Needs Provision in Global Contexts.* Routledge Taylor &Francis Group: London and New York.

Groźna iluzja inkluzji – edukacja włączająca jako metoda na dekonstrukcję oświaty [The Dangerous Illusion of Inclusion – Inclusive Education as a Method for Deconstructing Education]. (2022). Downloaded from: http://solidarni2010.pl/42377-pch24pl-grozna-il uzja-inkluzji--edukacja-wlaczajaca-jako-metoda-na dekonstrukcje-oswiaty.html (October 2022).

Guillemot. F., Lacroix. F., & Nocus. I. (2022). Teachers' attitude towards inclusive education from 2000 to 2020: An extended meta-analysis. *International Journal of Educational Research Open*, 3, 100175.

Hajisoteriou. C., & Sorkos. G. (2022). Towards a new paradigm of "Sustainable Intercultural and inclusive education": A comparative "blended" approach. *Education Inquiry*, 1–17.

Hashmi. S., Khan. I. K., & Khanum. N. (2017). Inclusive education in government primary schools: Teacher perceptions. *Journal of Education and Educational Development*, 4(1), 32–47.

Hinz. A. (2009). Inklusive Pädagogik in der Schule–veränderter Orientierungsrahmen für die schulische Sonderpädagogik!? Oder doch deren Ende. *Zeitschrift für Heilpädagogik*, 60(5), 171–179.

Hodkinson. A. (2007). Inclusive Education and the Cultural Representation of Disability and Disabled People: Recipe for Disaster or Catalyst of Change?: An Examination of Non-Disabled Primary School Children's Attitudes to Children with Disabilities. *Research in Education*, 77(1), 56–76.

Hornby. G. (2014). *Inclusive Special Education. Evidence-Based Practices for Children with Special Needs and Disabilities*. Springer: New York.

Hornby. G. (2020). *The Necessity for Coexistence of Equity and Excellence in Inclusive and Special Education*. PRINTED FROM the OXFORD RESEARCH ENCYCLOPEDIA, EDUCATION (oxfordre.com/education). (c) Oxford University Press USA, 2020. All Rights Reserved. Personal use only; commercial use is strictly prohibited (for details see Privacy Policy and Legal Notice), 1–16.

Hwang. Y., Evans. D. (2011). Attitudes Towards Inclusion: Gaps Between Belief and Practice. *International Journal of Special Education*, 26 (1), 136–146.

Jachimczak. B. (2021). Edukacja włączająca w kontekstach szkolnych i społecznych w czasach „niepewności" [Inclusive Education in School and Social Contexts at a Time of "Uncertainty"]. *Pedagogika Społeczna Nova* [*Social Pedagogy Nova*], 1(2), 29–43.

Jachimczak. B., & Podgórska-Jachnik. D. (2023). *Edukacja włączająca w perspektywie i zadaniach samorządu terytorialnego* [*Inclusive Education in the Perspective and Tasks of Local Self-Government Authorities*]. Łódź – Warszawa: Wydawnictwo Uniwersytetu Łódzkiego – ORE.

Jałowiecki. B., Karpalski. S. (2011). Peryferia i pogranicza jako interdyscyplinarny obszar badawczy [Periphery and Borderlands as an Interdisciplinary Research Area] (7–30), In: B. Jałowiecki, S. Karpalski (eds.), *Peryferia i pogranicza. O potrzebie różnorodności* [*Periphery and Borderlands. On the Need for Diversity*]. Warszawa: Scholar.

Janiszewska-Nieścioruk. Z. (2016). (Nie)dojrzałość proinkluzyjnych zmian w kształceniu osób z niepełnosprawnością [(Im)Maturity of Pro-Inclusive Changes in Education of Persons with Disabilities]. *Niepełnosprawność. Dyskursy Pedagogiki Specjalnej* [*Disability. Discourses of Special Pedagogy*], 22, 47–59.

Jarosz. E. (2013). O potrzebie demokratyzowania polskiej szkoły. Czas na krok następny – podmiotowość i współudział dzieci w edukacji [On the Need to Democratise Polish Schools. Time for the Next Step – Subjectivity and Joint Participation of Children in Education], *Studia Edukacyjne* [*Educational Studies*], 2013, 49–60.

Johnson. J. B., Reynolds. H. T., & Mycoff. J. D. (2015). *Political Science Research Methods*. Los Angeles: CQ Press.

Jurkowski. S., & Mueller. B. (2018). Co-teaching in inclusive classes: The development of multi-professional cooperation in teaching dyads. *Teaching and Teacher Education*, 75, 224–231.

Kochanowska. E. (2015). Samoocena nauczycieli w zakresie kompetencji diagnostycznych i pracy z dziećmi ze specjalnymi potrzebami edukacyjnymi na etapie edukacji wczesnoszkolnej [Self-Assessment of Teachers with Regard to Diagnostic Competencies and Work with Children with Special Education Needs at Primary School Levels 1 to 3]. *Niepełnosprawność. Dyskursy Pedagogiki Specjalnej* [*Disability. Discourses of Special Pedagogy*], 20, 143–153.

Kołodziejczyk. R. (2020). Gotowość nauczycieli do pracy w systemie edukacji włączającej [Teachers' Readiness to Work in an Inclusive Education System]. *Lubelski Rocznik Pedagogiczny* [*Lublin Pedagogical Yearbook*], 12 (48), 125–142.

Krause. A., Muchacka. B., Przybyliński. S. (2017). Kształcenie nauczycieli – analiza na podstawie eksperckich doświadczeń z ocen programowych i instytucjonalnych Polskiej Komisji Akredytacyjnej [Teacher Education – Analysis Based on Expert Experiences from Curriculum and Institutional Assessments of the Polish Accreditation Commission]. *Lubelski Rocznik Pedagogiczny* [*Lublin Pedagogical Yearbook*], 40 (1), 89–103.

Kruk-Lasocka. J. (2012). *Dostrzec dziecko z perspektywy edukacji włączającej* [*Recognising the Child from the Point of View of Inclusive Education*]. Wrocław: Wydawnictwo Naukowe Dolnośląskiej Szkoły Wyższej.

Kurniawati. F., Minnaert. A., Mangunsong. F. Ahmed. W. (2012). Empirical Study on Primary School teachers' Attitudes Towards Inclusive Education in Jakarta, Indonesia. *Procedia-Social and Behavioral Sciences* 69, 1430–1436.

Kwestionariusz samooceny pracy szkoły, wersja polska [*Raising Achievement Self-Review, Polish version*]. (2020). Downloaded from: https://www.ore.edu.pl/2021/11/analiza-pr aktyki-szkolnej-i-charakterystyka-szkoly-efektywnie-realizujacej-edukacje-wlaczajaca -w-praktyce-raport-z-badan/ (September 2023). The tool was developed as part of European Agency projects and made available under a Creative Commons licence; the licence terms are available at: CC BY-NC-SA 4.0 Deed | Uznanie autorstwa-Użycie niekomercyjne-Na tych samych warunkach 4.0 Międzynarodowe | Creative Commons.

Lechta. V. (2016). Inkluzivní pedagogika základní determinanty (25–40). In: V. Lechta (ed.), *Inkluzivní pedagogika*. Portál: Praha.

Lindner. K. T., Schwab. S., Emara. M., & Avramidis. E. (2023). Do teachers favor the inclusion of all students? A systematic review of primary schoolteachers' attitudes towards inclusive education. *European Journal of Special Needs Education,* 1–22.

Loreman. T. (2009). Straight talk about inclusive education. *CASS Connections,* 6(4), 43–47.

Loreman. T. (2017). *Pedagogy for Inclusive Education,* Oxford Research Encyclopedias, Education, 2017. Downloaded from: Pedagogy for Inclusive Education | Oxford Research Encyclopedia of Education (May 2022).

Loreman. T., Forlin. C., & Sharma. U. (2014). Measuring indicators of inclusive education: A systematic review of the literature. *International Perspectives on Inclusive Education,* 3, 165–187.

MacBeath. J., Galton. M., Steward. S., MacBeath, A. & Page. C. (2006). *The Costs of Inclusion: a study of inclusion policy and practice in English primary, secondary and special schools.* Cambridge: Victoire Press.

Mackenzie. S. (2007). A review of recent developments in the role of the SENCo in the UK. *British Journal of Special Education,* 4 (34), 212–218.

Madachowicz. K., Bilewicz. M. (2020). *Nauczyciel wczesnej edukacji wobec wyzwań pedagogiki inkluzyjnej* [*Primary School Levels 1 to 3 Teachers and the Challenges of Inclusive Pedagogy*]. Wydawnictwo Adam Marszałek: Toruń.

Mäller. O., Michalík. J., Vitáskova. K., Ludíková. L., Peutelschmiedová. A., Souralová. E., Dufková. P., Valenta. M., Grofková. I. (2004). *Dítě se speciální vzdělávacími potřebami v běžne škole*. Olomouci: Univerzita Palackěho v Olomuci.

Manifest Komunistyczny edukacji włączającej [*The Communist Manifesto of Inclusive Education*] (2022). Downloaded from: https://www.msn.com/pl-pl/wiadomosci/polska /droga-do-depopulacji-czym-jest-edukacja-w%C5%82%C4%85czaj%C4%85ca/ar-A A12POuM?ocid=entnewsntp&cvid=3a88390902ec4d2eb2b0ae330ee3cb38 (May 2023).

Marciniak-Madejska. N. (2014). Osoby z niepełnosprawnością na wsi – bariery integracji społecznej [Persons with Disabilities in Rural Areas – Barriers to Social Inclusion]. *Interdyscyplinarne Konteksty Pedagogiki Specjalnej* [*Interdisciplinary Contexts of Special Pedagogy*], 5, 51–67.

Markens. H. (2003). Badania podłużne [Longitudinal Studies]. In: E. Narkiewicz-Niedbalec, E. Hajduk, B. Idzikowski (eds.) *Człowiek i społeczeństwo w perspektywie zmiany społecznej. Polskie i niemieckie badania podłużne* [*Humans and the Society in the Perspective of Social Change. Polish and German Longitudinal Studies*] (17–26). Zielona Góra: Oficyna Wydawnicza Uniwersytetu Zielonogórskiego.

Mazurek. K., Winzer. M. A. (1994). (eds.), *Comparative special education*. Gallaudet University Press: Washington.

McGhie-Richmond. D., Irvine. A., Loreman. T., Cizman. J. L., and Lupar. J. (2013). Teacher Perspectives on Inclusive Education in Rural Alberta, Canada, *Canadian Journal of Education*, 36, 195–239.

MEiN planuje duże zmiany w edukacji. Nauczycielka: to jakaś farsa. (2021). Downloaded from: https://wiadomosci.onet.pl/kraj/szkoly-specjalne-czy-zostana-zlikwidowane-ed ukacja-wlaczajaca/49y1hll.

MEiN: W polskich szkołach i przedszkolach jest 187,9 tys. dzieci i młodzieży z Ukrainy, przybyłych po wybuchu wojny [*In Polish Schools and Pre-Schools, There Are 187,000 Children and Youth from Ukraine Who Arrived After the Outbreak of the War*]. (2023). Downloaded from: https://samorzad.pap.pl/kategoria/edukacja/mein-w-polskich-szko lach-i-przedszkolach-jest-1879-tys-dzieci-i-mlodziezy-z (July 2023).

Meng. D. (2008). The attitudes of primary school teachers toward inclusive education in rural and urban China. *Frontiers of Education in China*, 3(4), 473–492.

Mitchell. D. (2005). Introduction: Sixteen propositions on the contexts of inclusive education (1–21). D. Mitchell (ed.). *Contextualizing inclusive education. Evaluating old and new international perspectives*. London, New York: Routledge.

Mitchell. D. (2008). *What Really Works in Special Needs and Inclusive Education: Using Evidence-based Teaching Strategies?* London: Routledge.

Mitchell. D. (2016). Sprawdzone metody w edukacji specjalnej i włączającej. Gdańsk: Harmonia, Universalis. Translated by: J. Okuniewski.

Mitchell. D. (ed.) (2005). *Contextualizing inclusive education. Evaluating old and new international perspectives*. London, New York: Routledge.

Model edukacji dla wszystkich. Rozwiązania systemowe ukierunkowane na zapewnienie wysokiej jakości kształcenia, wychowania i opieki z uwzględnieniem zróżnicowania potrzeb rozwojowych i edukacyjnych dzieciom, uczniom i dorosłym osobom uczącym się

[*A Model of Education for All. Systemic Solutions Aimed at Providing High Quality Teaching, Education and Care Taking into Account Developmental and Educational Needs to Chldren, Pupils and Adult Learners*]. (2020). Warszawa: Ministerstwo Edukacji Narodowej. Downloaded from: https://www.gov.pl/web/edukacja-i-nauka/model-edu kacji-dla-wszystkich (November 2020).

Moltó. M. C. C. (2003). Mainstream teachers' acceptance of instructional adaptations in Spain. *European Journal of Special Needs Education,* 18(3), 311–332.

Monsen. J. J., Ewing. D. L., & Kwoka. M. (2014). Teachers' attitudes towards inclusion, perceived adequacy of support and classroom learning environment. *Learning environments research,* 17, 113–126.

Nikitorowicz. J. (2017). *Etnopedagogika w kontekście wielokulturowości i ustawicznie kształtującej się tożsamości* [*Ethno-pedagogy in the Context of Multiculturalism and Continuously Forming Identity*]. Impuls: Kraków.

Nowak. A. (2020). Edukacja włączająca w opiniach i ocenach nauczycieli: doniesienie z badań [Inclusive Education in Teachers' Opinions and Assessments: Research Report]. *Studia Pedagogiczne* [*Educational Studies*], 35, 169–181.

Okilwa. N. S., Jo Cordova. A., Haupert. K. (2022) Learning in a New Land: School Leadership in Support of Refugee Students, *Leadership and Policy in Schools,* 21 (3), 695–717.

Orakci. S., Aktan. O., Toraman. Ç., & Çevik. H. (2016). The Influence of Gender and Special Education Training on Attitudes Towards Inclusion. *International Journal of Instruction,* 9(2), 107–122.

Otukile-Mongwaketse. M., Mangope. B., & Kuyini. A. B. (2016). Teachers' understandings of curriculum adaptations for learners with learning difficulties in primary schools in Botswana: issues and challenges of inclusive education. *Journal of Research in Special Educational Needs, 16* (3), 169–177.

Paulsrud. D., & Nilholm. C. (2023). Teaching for inclusion–a review of research on the cooperation between regular teachers and special educators in the work with students in need of special support. *International Journal of Inclusive Education,* 27(4), 541–555.

Peng. Y., Potměšil. M. (2015). *Inclusive Setting – A Current Issue In Special Education.* Olomouc: Palacký University.

Pszczołowski. T. (1978). *Mała encyklopedia prakseologii i teorii organizacji* [*Concise Encyclopaedia of Organisational Theory and Praxeology*]. Wrocław, Warszawa, Kraków, Gdańsk: Zakład Narodowy im. Ossolińskich.

Pyżalski. J., Kata. G., Poleszak. W., Plichta. P. (2022). *Razem w klasie. Dzieci z Ukrainy w polskich szkołach. Potencjały i wyzwania w budowaniu wielokulturowej szkoły w kontekście wojny w Ukrainie według nauczycieli i nauczycielek. Raport z badania* [*Together in the Classroom. Children from Ukraine in Polish Schools. Potentials and Challenges in the Building of a Multicultural School in the Context of the War in Ukraine According to Teachers. Research Report*]. Warszawa: Fundacja Szkoła z klasą.

Rafał-Łuniewska. J. (2022). *Zróżnicowane potrzeby uczniów z Ukrainy. Jak na nie odpowiadać?* [*Diverse Needs of Learners from Ukraine. How to Respond to Them?*] Ośrodek Rozwoju Edukacji: Warszawa.

Reforma edukacji włączającej – obawy o szkody w całym systemie oświaty [*Inclusive Education Reform – Concerns About Damage to the Whole Educational System*] (2021). Downloaded from: https://www.prawo.pl/oswiata/likwidacja-szkol-specjalnych-eduka cja-wlaczajaca,507386.html (September 2023).

Reynolds. C. R., Flechter-Janzen. E. (eds.) (2002). *Concise Encyclopedia of Special Education. A Reference for the Education of the Handicapped and Other Exception Children and Adults.* New York: John Wiley & Sons.

Robinson. K., & Aronica. L. (2016). *Creative schools: The grassroots revolution that's transforming education.* New York: Penguin Books.

Romi. S., & Leyser. Y. (2006). Exploring inclusion preservice training needs: a study of variables associated with attitudes and self-efficacy beliefs. *European Journal of Special Needs Education,* 21(1), 85–105.

Ordinance of the Minister of Education and Science of 8 April 2022 amending the Ordinance on the Organisation of Teaching, Education and Care of Children and Youth Who Are Citizens of Ukraine. (2022). Dz. U. [Journal of Laws] 2022, item 795.

Ruch Ochrony Szkoły [School Protection Movement]. (2022). Downloaded from: https://ruchochronyszkoly.pl/ (July 2023).

Ryndak. D. L., Jackson. L., Billingsley. F. (2000). Defining School Inclusion for Students With Moderate to Severe Disabilities, What Do Experts Say? *Exceptionality,* 8(2), 101–116.

Sadowska. S. (2018). Projekt „szkoły dla wszystkich"– w poszukiwaniu wzorca działania i możliwości jego urzeczywistniania w polskich szkołach ["Schools for All" Project – In Search of a Model for Action and the Possibilities for its Implementation in Polish Schools]. *Niepełnosprawność. Dyskursy Pedagogiki Specjalnej [Disability. Discourses of Special Pedagogy],* 32, 38–56.

Saloviita. T. (2020). Teacher Attitudes Towards the Inclusion of Students with Support Needs. *Journal of Research in Special Educational Needs,* 20 (1), 64–73.

Savolainen. H., Engelbrecht. P., Nel. M., & Malinen. O. P. (2012). Understanding teachers' attitudes and self-efficacy in inclusive education: Implications for pre-service and in-service teacher education. *European Journal of Special Needs Education,* 27(1), 51–68.

Sawiński. Z. (2007). Badania trackingowe [Tracking Studies]. In: D. Mainson, A. Noga-Bogomilski: *Badania marketingowe. Od teorii do praktyki [Marketing Studies. From Theory to Pratice]* (103–118). Gdańsk: Gdańskie Wydawnictwo Psychologiczne.

Sharma. U., & Sokal. L. (2016). Can teachers' self-reported efficacy, concerns, and attitudes toward inclusion scores predict their actual inclusive classroom practices?. *Australasian Journal of Special Education,* 40(1), 21–38.

Sharma. U., Forlin. C., Deppeler. J. M., & Yang. G. (2013). Reforming teacher education for inclusion in developing countries in the Asia-Pacific region. *Asian Journal of Inclusive Education,* 1(1), 3–16.

Siódmy raport dotyczący sytuacji mniejszości narodowych i etnicznych oraz języka regionalnego w Rzeczypospolitej Polskiej [Seventh Report on the Situation of National and Ethnic Minorities and of Regional Language in the Republic of Poland]. (2020). Serwis Rzeczpospolitej Polskiej: Warszawa. Downloaded from: https://www.gov.pl/web/mniej szosci-narodowe-i-etniczne/vii-raport-ustawowy (July 2023).

Skibska. J. (2021). Postawy (przekonania) nauczycieli edukacji wczesnoszkolnej wobec edukacji inkluzyjnej – struktura badanego zjawiska [Attitudes (Beliefs) of Primary School Levels 1 to 3 Teachers Concerning Inclusive Education – Structure of the Phenomenon Studied]. *Niepełnosprawność. Dyskursy Pedagogiki Specjalnej [Disability. Discourses of Special Pedagogy],* 41, 32–147.

Skibska. J., Borzęcka. A., Twaróg-Kanus. A. (2020). *Kompetencje diagnostyczne i ter-apeutyczne w percepcji nauczycieli szkół ogólnodostępnych, integracyjnych i specjalnych* [*Diagnostic and Therapeutic Competencies as Perceived by Mainstream, Inclusive and Special School Teachers*]. Impuls: Kraków.

Skotnicka. B. (2019). *Przygotowanie szkoły wiejskiej do edukacji inkluzyjnej* [*Preparing a Rural School for Inclusive Education*]. Wydawnictwo Uniwersytetu Kazimierza Wiel-kiego: Bydgoszcz.

Slee. R. (2004). Social justice and the changing directions in educational research: the case of inclusive education (77–78). In: D. Mitchell (ed.), *Special Educational Needs and Inclusive Education.* Vol. II. Inclusive Education. London and New York: Routledge-Falmer.

Slee. R. (2011). *The irregular school: Exclusion, schooling, and inclusive education.* Ab-bingdon, UK: Routledge.

Slee. R. (2011). *The irregular school: Exclusion, schooling, and inclusive education.* Ab-bingdon, UK: Routledge.

Slee. R. (2014). Discourses of inclusion and exclusion: Drawing wider margins. *Power and education,* 6 (1), 7–17.

Sołoma. L. (2002). *Metody i techniki badań socjologicznych. Wybrane zagadnienia* [*Methods and Techniques of Sociological Studies. Selected Aspects*]. Olsztyn: Wy-dawnictwo Uniwersytetu Warmińsko-Mazurskiego.

Soylu. A., Kaysılı. A., Sever. M. (2020). Refugee Children and Adaptation to School: An Analysis through Cultural Responsivities of the Teachers. *Education and Science,* 45, 313–334.

Special Education. (2020). PRINTED FROM the OXFORD RESEARCH ENCYCLOPEDIA, EDUCATION (oxfordre.com/education). (c) Oxford University Press USA, 2020. All Rights Reserved. Personal use only; commercial use is strictly prohibited (for details see Privacy Policy and Legal Notice), 1–16.

Speck. O. (2013). *Inkluzja edukacyjna a pedagogika lecznicza* [*Educational Inclusion and Therapeutic Pedagogy*]. Harmonia Universalis:. Gdańsk.

Spendel. Z. (1991). Rozważania nad ludzką podmiotowością [Reflections on Human Subjectivity]. *Folia Philosophica,* 8, 47–61.

Świątkiewicz-Mośny. M. (2014). Źle, źle wszystko źle – o reformowaniu polskiej szkoły: analiza materiałów prasowych dotyczących zmian w oświacie w roku 2012 [Wrong, Wrong, All Wrong – On Reforming Polish Schools: Anaysis of Press Materials Con-cerning Changes in Education in 2012]. In: A. Rzymełka-Frąckiewicz (ed.) *Współczesna szkoła w następstwie przemian społeczno-kulturowych. Studia i refleksje socjopedago-giczne* [*Contemporary Schools in the Aftermath of Sociocultural Transformations. So-ciopedagogical Studies and Reflections*] (31–41). Toruń: Akapit.

Syrnyk. M. (2017). Polityka oświatowa wobec migrantów – uczniowie z Ukrainy w polskiej szkole [Educational Policy Towards Migrants – Learners from Ukraine in Polish Schools]. *Acta Politica Polonica,* 40, 53–72.

Szaban. D. (2020). Transfer kulturowy [Cultural Transfer] (438–446). In: E. Opiłowska, M. Dębicki, K. Dolińska. J. Kajta. Z. Kurcz. N. Niedźwiecka-Iwańczak. (eds.), (2020). *Studia nad granicami i pograniczami* [*Border and Borderland Studies*]. Scholar: Warszawa.

Sztompka. P. (2012). *Socjologia. Analiza społeczeństwa* [*Sociology. Analysis of Society*]. Kraków: Znak.

Szumski. G. (2019). Koncepcje edukacji włączającej [Concepts of Inclusive Education]. In: I. Chrzanowska, G. Szumski (eds.), *Edukacja włączająca w przedszkolu i szkole [Inclusive Education in Pre-Schools and Schools]* (15–24). Warszawa: FRSE.

Szumski. G., & Firkowska-Mankiewicz, A. (2010). *Wokół edukacji włączającej: efekty kształcenia uczniów z niepełnosprawnością intelektualną w stopniu lekkim w klasach specjalnych, integracyjnych i ogólnodostępnych [Around Inclusive Education: Effects of Teaching Learners with Mild Intellectual Disabilities in Special, Inclusive and Mainstream Classrooms]*. Warszawa: Wydawnictwo Akademii Pedagogiki Specjalnej.

Szumski. G., Smogorzewska. J., Narkun. Z., & Trębacz-Ritter. A. (2021). Współnauczanie i jego znaczenie dla procesu edukacji. Przegląd badań [Co-teaching and Its Importance for the Education Process. Research Review]. *Niepełnosprawność. Dyskursy Pedagogiki Specjalnej [Disability. Discourses of Special Pedagogy]*, 44, 76–97.

Thomas. G., Loxley. A. (2007). *Deconstructing Special Education and Constructing Inclusion,* New York: Open University Press.

Thomazet. S. (2009). From Integration to Inclusive Education: Does Changing the Terms Improve Practice? *The International Journal of Inclusive Education,* 13 (6), 553–563.

Tissot. C. (2013). The role of SENCos as leaders. *British Journal of Special Education,* 1 (40), 33–40.

Topping. K. & Maloney. S. (2005). Introduction (1–14) K. Topping & S. Maloney (eds.), *The Routledge Falmer Reader in Inclusive Education.* London: Routledge.

Wagner. J. (2018). *Struggling for Educational Justice in Disabling Societies: A Multi-sited School-based Ethnography of Inclusive Policies and Practices in Poland, Austria and Germany.* Doctoral dissertation Wroclaw: Lower Silesian University of Education.

Walton. E. (2018). Decolonising (Through) Inclusive Education? *Educational Research for Social Change,* 7 (0), 31–45.

Werner. S., Gumpel. T. P., Koller. J., Wiesenthal. V., & Weintraub. N. (2021). Can self-efficacy mediate between knowledge of policy, school support and teacher attitudes towards inclusive education? *PloS one,* 16 (9), e0257657.

Wiśniewska. E. (2016). Przywództwo edukacyjne nauczyciela [Teachers' Educational Leadership]. *Społeczeństwo. Edukacja. Język [Society. Education. Language]*, 4, 103–113.

Zacharuk. T. (2008). *Wprowadzenie do edukacji inkluzyjnej [An Introduction to Inclusive Education]*. Siedlce: Wydawnictwo Akademii Podlaskiej.

Zamkowska. A. (2004). *Systemy kształcenia integracyjnego w wybranych krajach Unii Europejskiej [Inclusive Education Systems in Selected European Union Countries]*. Wydawnictwo Politechniki Radomskiej: Radom.

Zamkowska. A. (2009). *Wsparcie edukacyjne uczniów z upośledzeniem umysłowym w stopniu lekkim w różnych formach kształcenia na I etapie edukacji [Educational Support of Learners with Mild Intellectual Disabilities in Various Forms of Teaching at the First Stage of Education]*. Radom: Wydawnictwo Politechniki Radomskiej.

Zamkowska. A. (2017). Kształtowanie kultury szkoły włączającej –z doświadczeń zagranicznych [Shaping an Inclusive School Culture – A Selection of Experiences from Abroad]. *Niepełnosprawność – zagadnienia, problemy, rozwiązania [Disability – Aspects, Problems, Solutions]*, 11(24), 59–68.

Żuraw. H. (2016). Wizerunek dziecka z zaburzeniami rozwoju w poglądach nauczycieli szkół masowych [Children with Developmental Disorders as Viewed by Mainstream

School Teachers]. *Lubelski Rocznik Pedagogiczny* [*Lublin Pedagogical Yearbook*], XXXV, (3), 75–106.

Żyta. A., Byra. S., & Ćwirynkało. K. (2017). Education of children and youth with disabilities in Poland and the UN Convention on the Rights of Persons with Disabilities. *Hrvatska Revija za Rehabilitacijska Istrazivanja*, 53, 244–251.

Annex

Raising Achievement Self-Review. Self-review survey

The self-review survey is an open educational resource. This means it is a learning resource that is 'usable, adaptable to specific learning needs, and shareable freely' (European Commission, 2013). Users are free to adapt, modify and re-purpose it as required, providing a reference to the original source is given.

Data protection statement

All the data collected in this survey will be held anonymously and securely.

Instructions for completing the survey

Section 1 asks for some background information on your role. Section 2 has a number of statements about the issue of inclusive pedagogy. Section 3 has a number of statements about school leadership.

For Sections 2 and 3, please rate your level of agreement with each of the statements using a 5-point scale:
- Strongly agree
- Agree
- Unsure
- Disagree
- Strongly disagree.

Mark the relevant box to indicate the option that most closely describes your level of agreement. Please only select one answer per row.

There are 68 statements – please reply to them all.

The survey should take around 20 minutes to complete.

Section 1 – Background information

This section asks for some background information on your role in your learning community (LC).

How would you describe your role in your LC?
- School leadership team member   ___
- Class/subject teacher   ___
- Support personnel   ___
- Parent   ___
- Other (please specify and briefly describe your role)   _____

Section 2 – Inclusive pedagogy

This section looks at two key issues relating to classroom-level practice (Pedagogy for all learners and Support for learning). Each issue has a number of statements for you to rate.

Please answer all questions. Please only select one answer per row.

Pedagogy for all learners

These statements focus on teachers' attitudes to diversity and their knowledge and understanding of the teaching and learning process which affects the approaches they use to assess and personalise learning.

Statements	Strongly agree	Agree	Unsure	Disagree	Strongly disagree
Teachers take responsibility for the learning of all learners in their classes					
Teachers act to address the diverse requirements of all learners in their classes					
Teachers interact with learners sensitively and respectfully					
Teachers have high expectations for all learners					
Teachers use research evidence to support decisions about innovative approaches to learning					
Teachers help learners to think about their own learning processes and strategies					

(Continued)

Statements	Strongly agree	Agree	Unsure	Disagree	Strongly disagree
Teachers personalise learning for all learners					
Teachers use flexible groupings (e.g. whole class, small groups, pair) to enable learners to interact and access multiple perspectives					
Teachers use a range of learning resources and technologies to enhance learning					
Teachers offer learners a range of ways to show what they have learned					
Teachers use formative assessment to enable learners to plan the next steps in their learning					
Teachers give feedback focused on effort and progress					

Support for learning

This section is designed to look at the ways that teachers support learners who are underachieving or who may have particular requirements – including how they collaborate with colleagues.

Statements	Strongly agree	Agree	Unsure	Disagree	Strongly disagree
All stakeholders recognise vulnerable learners' right to support and reasonable adjustments					
Teachers use a range of assessment methods to support their judgements about the need for adjustments or additional resources at classroom level					
Teachers use a range of approaches/strategies to provide additional support for learners when necessary (e.g. universal design, peer support, mentoring)					
Teachers use appropriate resources and technologies to improve access to learning					

(Continued)

Statements	Strongly agree	Agree	Unsure	Disagree	Strongly disagree
Teachers collaborate and plan with other staff/professionals to meet individual learner requirements					
Teacher roles are flexible (e.g. specialised teachers and general/subject teachers can work interchangeably in the classroom)					
Teachers contribute to formal assessments at school/local area level (e.g. for a statement/certificate of special educational needs)					
There are procedures to identify underachievement and address any factors that affect learning as soon as they arise					

Section 3 – Leadership and collaboration

This section looks at five key issues relating to school-level practice (Leadership roles and approaches, Learner well-being and participation, Curriculum development, Partnerships and collaborative working, and Support systems for staff and leaders). Each issue has a number of statements for you to rate.

Please answer all questions. Please only select one answer per row.

Leadership roles and approaches

This section focuses on how school leaders (head teachers/principals) work with others to establish a positive school atmosphere and climate. This includes providing leadership for learning, focusing on equity and using information for improvement.

Statements	Strongly agree	Agree	Unsure	Disagree	Strongly disagree
Leaders use a collaborative process to develop a shared vision and inclusive values					
Leaders encourage strong, trusting relationships					

(Continued)

Statements	Strongly agree	Agree	Unsure	Disagree	Strongly disagree
Leaders facilitate effective communication between all stakeholders (e.g. staff, learners, parents, other professionals, community members)					
Leaders are pro-active in managing change and dealing with uncertainty					
Leaders involve all stakeholders in decision-making					
Leaders develop a climate/culture in which all learners are known and treated as individuals					
Leaders see inclusion as central to school improvement					
Leaders use data to monitor and evaluate practice and impact on all learners					
Leaders use research evidence to plan improvement					
Leaders focus on learning to raise the aspirations and achievement of all learners					
Leaders ensure that all stakeholders understand the assessment processes used in school and how such information might be used (e.g. formative assessment for learning/summative assessment for reporting)					
Leaders monitor equity of access to the full range of learning opportunities and school activities					

Learner well-being and participation

These statements consider the school's approach to learner well-being (including the development of a growth mindset) and the extent to which learners are listened to and enabled to take part in all learning and wider activities.

Statements	Strongly agree	Agree	Unsure	Disagree	Strongly disagree
All staff take responsibility for learner well-being, seeing it as central to learner success					
All staff see learner diversity as an asset to the school					
The school provides support to reduce any barriers to learner attendance (e.g. bullying, family circumstances)					
All staff encourage positive relationships between peers					
The school culture enables all learners to feel that they 'belong'					
The learner voice is central to the school community (daily operation and on-going improvement)					
All staff encourage learners to see mistakes as learning opportunities					
All staff support learners to participate in the full range of learning opportunities/activities					
All staff encourage independence and self-advocacy in learners					
Procedures for dealing with discriminatory language and attitudes are always followed					
Conflict/incidents of bullying are acted on promptly					
Learners can communicate with staff about personal issues that affect their learning					

Curriculum development

These statements focus on how the school implements the national curriculum or plans its own curriculum to provide relevant and engaging opportunities for all learners.

Statements	Strongly agree	Agree	Unsure	Disagree	Strongly disagree
The school has an agreed curriculum framework that takes account of principles such as breadth, balance, coherence and relevance					
The school curriculum provides valued learning opportunities for all learners					
The school curriculum provides flexibility for teachers to plan authentic and challenging learning opportunities for all learners					
The school curriculum provides opportunities for learners to make choices about their own learning programmes					
The school curriculum framework addresses learner well-being as a priority					
The school curriculum supports effective transition between phases/settings					
Extra-curricular and community activities are planned to engage all learners					
The assessment framework provides opportunities to recognise wider achievement (e. g. social, sporting, artistic), as well as academic attainment					

Partnerships and collaborative working

These statements consider the school's work with parents/families and with the wider community – that aims to raise learner aspirations and achievement.

Statements	Strongly agree	Agree	Unsure	Disagree	Strongly disagree
The school provides accessible information to promote inclusive education to parents and the wider community					

(Continued)

Statements	Strongly agree	Agree	Unsure	Disagree	Strongly disagree
The school works closely with parents to raise the aspirations and achievement of all learners					
The school welcomes families into school to discuss issues that are important to them					
Input from parents/families is a valued part of decision-making and advocacy activities					
The school networks with other local schools, colleges, universities and workplaces to provide a wider range of opportunities for learners					
The school works in partnership with other agencies (e. g. health, social services) to provide additional support for learners when necessary					
All stakeholders are clear about their own roles in the school and the roles and contributions of others					
External stakeholders/partners have a role in reviewing/validating school self-evaluation activities					

Support systems for staff and leaders

The statements look at support systems within the school community for staff and for school leaders.

Statements	Strongly agree	Agree	Unsure	Disagree	Strongly disagree
Staff are supported to engage with 'hard-to-reach' families					
Staff are encouraged to take part in development opportunities that will improve learning and achievement in the school community					
Staff are supported to share learning and reflect with colleagues as a form of professional development					

(Continued)

Statements	Strongly agree	Agree	Unsure	Disagree	Strongly disagree
Staff are given leadership opportunities (e. g. taking a lead on new initiatives/curriculum areas)					
Staff can access support for their own well-being in times of stress					
Leaders are supported by colleagues within the school					
Leaders receive support from external partners/networks (e. g. other school and community leaders, university colleagues)					
Leaders receive appropriate training to promote school development with a focus on positive outcomes for all learners					